Praise for *The Invisible*  KU-303-856

'*The Invisible Woman* speaks to me, and for me. It's about saying "up yours" to the cult of youth, but also about seeing the life of the 50+ as hilariously funny (not unlike the life of the 15 year-old, when you come to think about it).'

Mary Beard

'*The Invisible Woman* … reminds us that style and wit begin in youth but are mastered in middle age. You can roundly stick your 20s. Hers is a voice for proper grown-ups not yet ready to come down, and I'm in.'

Alison Moyet

'Stylish and wittily written, it's a brilliant read that should encourage us all to challenge the cult of youth, and learn to love ourselves a little more along the way.'

My Weekly

'*The Invisible Woman* [is] a warm, companionable book with a tart aftertaste.'

Guardian

'We love the way Helen writes. She tells it as it is because she KNOWS how it is. At Gransnet we constantly battle against the misconceptions and prejudices around ageing. We are delighted that Helen is helping to set the record straight and embrace her philosophies wholeheartedly and with gusto.'

Gransnet

'I immediately wanted to give it to someone in their early 40s to say "Look! this next bit can be challenging but it's also great fun!" Written in her funny and frank style it's a joy and full of properly useful words of wisdom.'

Room

'Helen Walmsley-Johnson has a gift for writing, and she tells it like it is with great humour … I urge you to buy it for yourself and give a copy to all your fifty-something friends!'

The Good Book Guide

'A funny look at those of a certain age who are fed up with being overlooked.'

Good Housekeeping

THE Invisible Woman

Taking on the Vintage Years

HELEN WALMSLEY-JOHNSON

ICON

First published in the UK in 2015
by Icon Books Ltd, Omnibus Business Centre,
39–41 North Road, London N7 9DP
email: info@iconbooks.com
www.iconbooks.com

This edition published in the UK in 2016 by Icon Books Ltd

Sold in the UK, Europe and Asia
by Faber & Faber Ltd, Bloomsbury House,
74–77 Great Russell Street,
London WC1B 3DA or their agents

Distributed in the UK, Europe and Asia
by Grantham Book Services, Trent Road,
Grantham NG31 7XQ

Distributed in Australia and New Zealand
by Allen & Unwin Pty Ltd,
PO Box 8500, 83 Alexander Street,
Crows Nest, NSW 2065

Distributed in South Africa
by Jonathan Ball, Office B4, The District,
41 Sir Lowry Road, Woodstock 7925

Distributed in India
by Penguin Books India,
7th Floor, Infinity Tower – C, DLF Cyber City,
Gurgaon 122002, Haryana

ISBN: 978-178578-052-3

Typeset in Janson Text by Marie Doherty

Printed and bound in the UK
by Clays Ltd, St Ives plc

Contents

ABOUT THE AUTHOR

Helen Walmsley-Johnson is a freelance writer and author of the *Guardian*'s popular online style column, 'The Vintage Years'. She also writes for the *New Statesman*, *The Pool* and *Standard Issue* magazine. With a particular interest in feminist issues and the rights of older women, Helen has spoken out against ageism and domestic abuse on *Woman's Hour*, BBC Radio and BBC Breakfast. She lives in a village in Rutland.

Introduction

'Old age is no place for sissies'
—BETTE DAVIS

This is a book about ageing. Specifically it is a book about women and late middle age. I am middle-aged (there, I said it) and since you're reading this, I suspect you might be too. If I'm truthful, I was mostly through my middle age and out the other side before I even accepted that I *was* middle-aged. In this you and I may find we have a certain amount in common. You perhaps also share my frustration at the general lack of information, the attitudes of the media (mainly) and others (generally), and at the way we are portrayed – all of which add to a slight feeling of unease, which begins to make itself part of everyday life. A faint sense of dread at the onset of middle age is entirely understandable, although we'd probably be better to call it what it is – fear. Fear that 'life' as we know it is over, fear for the future and fear of the unknown. Middle age has become the uncharted grey bit on life's map, the *terra incognita* wasteland we must navigate before we can get on with being properly old. When we're old we hope we'll know who and what we are; the bit that gets us there is much harder to determine.

Let me start with a question or two. Would you place yourself with the 'drag me kicking and screaming into retirement' middle agers, or are you one of the 'thank God *that's* all over and I can put my feet up for a bit' group? Or perhaps you're one of the women who at some point in the last decade wandered unintentionally up an economic cul-de-sac and spend days and nights wringing their hands and worrying about how they're going to struggle through to the relative security of a state pension.

There's a lot of noise made by the Middle Age Resistance. They're the ones tearing about with their sports cars and motorbikes, the ones flouting every age-conscious style rule in the book; they're the ones who backpack around the world on their children's inheritance and pop up on your telly and in your newspapers pulling, God help us, 'wacky' stunts; they're the rowdy groovers at Glastonbury having loud thrice-nightly sex under canvas; they're the ones who resist, resist, resist and vow to go down in a blaze of glory shouting, 'Look at me – nothing middle-aged here!' Meanwhile the accepters are quietly, and perhaps a tad smugly, getting on with kicking back, shooting the breeze and being, well, *middle-aged* but in the more conventional sense as we are given to understand it, comfortably cocooned in their mortgage-free, pension-savvy world with the drawbridge firmly up ('Crisis? What crisis?') and accepting this latest life stage with equanimity and quiet resignation. Apparently.

Why is this age group presented as polar opposites, aggressively divided on the 'right' and 'wrong' ways to grow older? What of the ones who have no option but to grit their teeth and get on with life as they always have but find the age cards stacked against them? Why does the media always depict the middle-aged gilded with comfortable privilege? Isn't there a case for a fresh look at middle age? There is growing interest in this further transitional phase of life and it provides us with an opportunity to position it as something more interesting, less frightening and as something concerned not with loss but with gain; a chance to redraw outdated concepts of beauty; to appreciate wisdom and experience; as a more comfortable mix of resisting the depredations of an ageing mind and body while also gracefully accepting and embracing the inevitability of it? There is a case to be made for preparing for middle age – physically, mentally and financially – and, during middle age, preparing for the old age that will follow … if we're lucky.

Even the *Oxford English Dictionary* herds middle agers together with a definition of 'the period of life between young adulthood and old age, now usually regarded as between 45 and 60' – a stark definition of fifteen years that feels like quite a stretch; there's a huge physical and psychological difference between a 45-year-old and a 60-year-old; just as there is between a 20-year-old and a 35-year-old at the other end of the age spectrum. It's simply not helpful to lump the whole group together.

In any case, I doubt many 45-year-olds think of themselves as middle-aged, I know I didn't. Nor did I wake up one morning and think 'here it is'. Middle age arrived in me – roughly five years later than the *OED* definition

– like puberty, with spurts, *longueurs* and occasional tears. At times I would be completely, stormily, at sea while at others I felt in an odd state of languid, drifting suspension. I would describe where I am now as battle-weary contentment. 'Contentment' is a word not much heard in relation to middle age and I've had to find my way through a fair few dense thickets of self-doubt, melting confidence and spitting rage at a world that won't fight with me to achieve it.

I wonder if any other age group is subjected to quite so much ill-defined and random generalisation. Take the popular misconception that, say by 50, you will have achieved what you're going to achieve – you will have had your shot at life, your best is behind you and now it's time to accept that you should drift quietly and without fuss or protest towards retirement. That is what we're told and, whatever we ourselves believe, there's a large chunk of society who do indeed think that by the time we're 50 we middle agers have zipped up the well-lit motorway of earlier life, bounced over the junction at the top and are now at least halfway down the B-road on the other side with no brakes, no lights, bad eyesight and a shaky grip on the steering wheel. Do I accept that? No, absolutely not. To continue the metaphor, I'm doing my damnedest to stay right there on the road, but I'm also adjusting my speed to take into account the age of my engine and bodywork.

The 'young-ist' culture of television, radio and the rest of the media has, for the most part, already consigned middle agers to a life less interesting and a road less travelled. What arrogance to prematurely chivvy us off into a routine of afternoon naps and daytime television! Speaking for myself – and while admitting to a slight fondness for a post-prandial snooze – I'm still working my socks off. We, the middle-aged, have so much to offer. We must assert our right to make plans, be heard, have interesting, useful lives. Historically middle and old age is when one generation passes its wisdom on to the next – a useful and admirable tradition worth perpetuating if only we could regain our lost voice. We should not allow our opinions and experience to be dismissed, however benignly, and we should not allow ourselves to be ignored. We should decide for ourselves what we want to do and when we want to do it, and we should fight to restore dignity and usefulness to this forgotten age. Isn't that just as important as the right to have pink hair, wear Doc Martens or ride a Harley Davidson? I do not accept this 'writing off'. I do not accept invisibility.

For me personally, the past few years have been a period of discovery – the discovery that contrary to received media wisdom I am still in possession of a fully functioning brain and still have the intelligence to put up a convincing argument; that while I can still be perved at from a passing car I can also suffer ageist abuse in a busy London street in broad daylight; and that I am perfectly capable of navigating my own solitary way from London to the South of France by train without being mugged or getting lost. Nonetheless, the day came when I ticked the 'age 55 to 64' box on a survey form and it struck me quite forcefully that I had at last become a proper grown-up and was officially middle-aged. Not a welcome moment if I'm honest – does anyone truly look forward to getting old? But the moment also came with a certain sense of ... achievement. Against all the odds I have survived this far. As moments go, it was pretty profound; it was one of those moments that make you stop and think for a bit about life. I'm one of the fortunate ones: I feel strong and healthy, I feel reasonably hopeful and, dare I say it, I feel an exciting little thrill of possibility, an opening up of new horizons. Despite my recent battering in one of life's storms, I feel *cautiously* optimistic.

On the other hand (for such is the seesawing of emotion that accompanies this time of life) I also feel a tad miserable, a touch apprehensive and quite a lot fed up, largely because the 'age 55 to 64' box is also the last-but-one box; it is the God's waiting room of my form-filling life. My limited ration of optimism is nibbled down further when most of what I read, watch or listen to about middle age is either patronising, reinforces the popular misconception of a slow decline, or is a broad comedy generalisation; in addition, over the last couple of years I've seen a new kid on the block of ageist debate – the 'them' versus 'us' argument. This is the one that says the older generation is robbing the younger one of its future; that we selfishly live in overly large houses, hog jobs and are unfairly protected against times of economic hardship. There's barely a week that goes by without me going nuclear about something or other to do with middle age as portrayed in the media. It seems that for the over-50s each day brings the invention of some fresh new paranoia, either ours or someone else's. Ageing I can accept as inevitable, but the way it is demonised, demeaned and ridiculed by the media is another matter. This helps no one. This I will fight ... this I will resist.

By now my personal list of annoyances would probably extend to several editions but, in its abridged form, it's this:

֍ Uncooperative and badly made clothing, such as tights, socks and t-shirts that twist when you put them on, shirt buttons that fall off and hems that drop on their first outing, anything that requires breathing in to do it up, etc., etc. I am no longer designed to wrestle with it, and I don't have the patience.

֍ The term 'age appropriate'. What *is* that?

֍ People who call me 'dear' or 'love' in any sense but the ironic.

֍ Telephones with large buttons of the type advertised in the back of certain magazines – see also walk-in baths, floral loose covers for my sofa, thermal knickers. Over my dead body.

֍ Callers to *You and Yours* and *Any Answers* on Radio 4 – occasionally I emerge from the fog of a radio-based rant with my hand reaching for the phone and I'm terrified that one day, possibly quite soon, I will turn into someone who telephones Radio 4.

§ Packaging – if tubs of soup were the only things standing between me and starvation I would die because I can never get the damn things open – see also tubs of vitamins, cocoa and toothbrushes.

§ Cheerful coffee shop staff – it's undignified. You do not know me and I do not know you. Let's keep it that way.

§ Mirrors all over the place in shops and department stores – my eyesight is not what it was and I'm apt to walk into things. I don't like what they show me either (a middle-aged woman with hair like a dormouse nest who may or may not be me. I don't know).

§ Fitting rooms in department stores – mainly for reasons of the cruel and merciless lighting but also because some bright young thing always whips the curtains open when I'm trying to pull up a pair of size 12 trousers over my size 14 backside. (A younger me would never have worried about this – she was a permanent size 8, goddammit.)

§ Hair flicking on public transport – hygiene and envy, pure and simple.

§ Young people in groups – because I now find them vaguely threatening and know that while I am still able to run I will not be able to run fast *enough*. Groups of young people must be passed silently, avoiding all eye contact.

§ Shop assistants or anyone else who makes assumptions without enquiry – just because my face says I'm middle-aged does not mean I want you to pigeonhole my wardrobe/menu choices/shoe requirements/understanding of modern technology, etc., etc. ad nauseam.

Given my sporadic rants and the way I feel about raising the profile of the middle-aged, I had no qualms at all about accepting an invitation to write a weekly column – 'The Vintage Years' – for the *Guardian* website. It began as a fairly straightforward idea – writing about style for older women – and has slowly become something more. At first, women were the ones reading and responding, but then a trickle of regular *male* readers began to add their two penn'orth to the discussion, which raised a set of other connected issues. When younger people chipped in with their own worries and anxieties about ageing, I began to realise that this 'problem' (if we choose to see it as such) of how we approach middle and old age is not restricted to those closest to it at all. If a young woman of 24 is already afraid about what will happen to her life and relationships as she begins to show signs of age, I think we have to acknowledge that there really is something wrong with the way we see the process of ageing and older people. It is, after all, an entirely natural process. Ageing is a physical process that needs to be accepted with serenity; we must learn to manage our expectations sensibly and not live in denial, or fight back with cosmetic surgery and treatments we can't afford, most of which just make us look weird. That we will all age is inevitable and inescapable but it doesn't alter the person we are inside; our character, memories, strength, personality and intelligence are what make us *us*. We are defined by our family and friends and those who care about us. How have we overlooked this and allowed a youth-obsessed media to cast the runes on our behalf? Without our steadying voices they have conjured a roiling, festering manifestation of age-related neuroses. Well done us.

With that in mind, it's perhaps not surprising that the pieces I write for the *Guardian* and others about what I, as a middle-aged woman, think and feel about getting older, and what it does to my sense of style and self, trigger far more debate than when I write a standard reporting piece from, say, London Fashion Week. I allow myself a degree of optimism at the reassuringly large appetite for discussion about ageing and how it affects us, both physically and psychologically. When the 'Vintage Years' column began, comments were, for the most part, from readers in the UK, but after a few weeks readers from around the world began to join in, voicing much the same anxieties whether they were in Sydney, Singapore, New York or Huddersfield. That in turn inspired me to start a Twitter account – @TheVintageYear – where I encouraged people to bat around thoughts and opinions in 140 characters (or fewer).

Eventually I tweeted this question to my followers: *What are the three things that worry you most about getting older?* I can tell you that it's comforting to discover that the same things are keeping all of us awake at night, irrespective of age, gender, nationality or income bracket. According to my poll the top three are:

1. Loss of health/memory/marbles
2. Loss of independence (via health or finances)
3. Loss of loved ones

Yes, it's all about loss.

Loss in today's acquisitive, goal-driven society can feel like defeat. This is true even of small, inevitable losses such as the loss of our youthful appearance. To accept our encroaching lines, wrinkles and grey hair has come to be regarded as some kind of personal failure – we are the losers, the defeated. But we'd be better off accepting this more superficial kind of loss. Time will inevitably steal from us anyway, but time also allows the blow to fall slowly, incrementally, and replaces what's gone with something else, if we have the courage to allow it. There are, after all, much worse things we may have to face – as recognised by my Twitter respondents.

Losing the people we love, for example, is a far heavier blow, probably the heaviest of all, but it is also the nature of love and life. To risk knowing love means we will know the grief of loss too and this is something that must also be accepted, although it is easier said than done and takes a great deal of time and effort. Fighting a few age spots (or are they freckles?) and laughter lines (or are they crow's feet?) pales into insignificance against the strength and courage required to endure close personal bereavement.

And then there are the other, more gentle losses, like the sweetly painful joy of seeing one's children grow into adults and leave the family home to build their own lives. This loss we must also accept but it is a loss tempered with pride, hopefully, at a job well done (and maybe just a little regret for the things we didn't do quite so well).

Conspicuously absent from that top three worries list, except inasmuch as it comes under 'loss of health', is the possibility of terminal illness. We don't discuss it, do we – in the same way we don't talk about death itself, or the unopened letter from HMRC on the sideboard. It's the elephant in the room; the haunting fear we dare not mention – as though to do so is to hand over a personal invitation for the Grim Reaper to join us for tea and biscuits on Wednesday week. And it doesn't help to think of life itself as terminal, which it is, or that the C-word (cancer) is quite commonly a disease of age. (In his book *The Emperor of All Maladies*, Siddhartha Mukherjee explains that 'cancer is built into our genomes' and that 'as we extend our life as a species, we inevitably unleash malignant growth' – further adding that 'mutations in cancer genes accumulate with aging; cancer is thus intrinsically related to age'.)

It's very strange that we avoid searching for facts when what scares us most of all is the unknown: the not-spoken-about hidden things. That's what makes us shout *Switch the bloody light on!* when someone in a film creeps down the dark, dark stairs to the dark, dark cellar with only a torch, a safety pin and a bar of soap. If we know, if we can see and understand what we're dealing with, wouldn't it go a long way to removing much of the fear? We really must be brave and stop being quite so squeamish about the things we'd rather not know because we're afraid of them. It's an entirely understandable and very common fear of something that is, after all, an undeniable fact of life (and, in the case of death itself, inevitable) so why do we do so little to address it? Is it that we can't find the information in accessible form, written in calm, straightforward language? And, by the way, you will eventually open that letter from HMRC and find it's nothing more threatening than your new tax code.

That brings us to that other worry – money, and the possibility of not having enough of it. In the spirit of honesty I must tell you that this is more likely than you might have supposed – the fabled 'grey pound' may not be quite as plentiful as we have been led to believe. According to research undertaken by Prudential, one in five retirees will retire into debt with an average monthly debt payment of £215. The trend is upwards, but as ever with our generation, there is a notable lack of useful data. Fortunately, our finances are one other thing we can work on to improve now, if we think and plan, take our heads out of the sand and refuse to accept what we're being palmed off with. It makes me very cross indeed that once you're past 50, and regardless of what's written into employment legislation, if you're looking for a change of career or just looking for a job, any job, the general perception is that as a middle-aged person you're past it; and that assumption will be made before anyone has even clapped eyes on you. How dare they?

From my own experience this prejudice is now countrywide and ubiquitous, although it used to be not so much of a problem inside London as outside it – and I base this observation on my relocation to London when I was 45 (officially middle-aged according to the outdated *OED*). In Leicestershire, where I'd lived much of my life, I was ambitious but unable to get so much as a sniff of any job commensurate with my experience and qualifications; London proved a much happier hunting ground ... then. However, a more recent job search proved frustrating (just shy of 500 applications resulting in only three interviews) and this, I discover, is a far from isolated experience for a fifty-something woman. In the capital what seems to be emerging is a narrowing of the white-collar recruitment pool at both ends of the age spectrum, with the youngest, least experienced applicants losing out at one extreme and the middle-aged candidates at the other. It's worth noting that between the first quarter of 2010 and the last quarter of 2013, unemployment among women aged 50–64 increased by 41 per cent from 108,000 to 152,000 nationwide. In comparison, unemployment in the same period among all people aged sixteen and over increased by just 1 per cent.* That current government statistics indicate otherwise would be, I suggest, more to do with the widespread use of controversial 'zero hours' contracts than anything else.

A date of birth may no longer go on to a CV but anyone with half a brain can work out a candidate's age from the other information it contains. It's hard to see this as anything other than age discrimination. You could make an argument that older people will expect salaries

---

* The Commission on Older Women, Interim Report, September 2013

commensurate with their experience, and this is what employers are wary of – but where does that leave the research cited in at least half-a-dozen of the reports currently in circulation that what older women need more than anything is flexibility? That, in other words, the salary is less important than having a choice about how you earn it? Reasonable hours of decently paid part-time work are the Holy Grail.

It seems the situation for the older jobseeker is just as desperate as it was when time was called on ageism by the Age Discrimination Act of 2006. If anything it's worse because the prejudice against and the unwillingness to employ an older worker is less in your face and more nuanced. The 'sits vac' is full of ads employing a variety of ambiguous words and phrases that provide an excellent smokescreen against prosecution, although it's quite clear what they're driving at. There is the phrase 'recent graduate', which is unlikely to be someone of 40-plus, much less someone in their 50s, or experience 'gained in a recent gap year' is mentioned. There are constant references to 'energetic', 'lively', 'demanding' and 'to fit in with a young team' – hinting at youthful enthusiasm and stamina rather than middle-aged stability and experience.

A lot is being made of older people becoming freelance or self-employed – the so-called 'olderpreneur'. Indeed, we are encouraged to choose that way but although we're very good at self-starting, it's a plan that does rather rely on having some start-up capital in the first place and it doesn't remove the problem of the persistent ageist attitude to older workers, which lies at the heart of so much of this issue. To say, as many reports do, that we are *choosing* to become self-employed is quite simply wrong. It is not a choice when it is our only option.

By 2020 over a third of the working population – and half the overall population – will be aged over 50. The retirement goalposts keep moving and as they inch ever nearer to 70 we're finding that all of us will have to work longer, which would be fine and dandy if there wasn't such ingrained prejudice towards us. We need to rethink the way our work in middle age prepares us for old age. My own observations seem to suggest that a great many of those earning the 'grey pound' will finish up minding a supermarket checkout.

And that's another problem right there – that at some point, and especially in tough economic times, we the middle-aged are expected to step aside and leave the field clear for the young – to which I would respond with two fingers held firmly and proudly aloft, reinforced with a concise verbal instruction in Anglo-Saxon. We, I, have a perfect right to employment but if we're to get it we have to conquer our aversion to showing off what we can do and blow our own trumpets quite a bit more than we do currently. After all, if we continue to work and earn then surely we're not the burden on society that pernicious propaganda suggests we are.

※

It's inspiring to see people doing brilliant, unpredictable things and especially when it's us, the middle-aged. Where are the stories of those of us who have chosen to go off and do a PhD in Advanced Nuclear Physics after spending the last 20 years working as a librarian, a train driver, a traffic warden, a doctor or an actor? Or perhaps a soldier who became a shepherd? Or a hairdresser who started up a cheese-making business? Perhaps we've had enough of working in an office and decide to open a restaurant. Or write a book. Why can't we hear and see middle-aged women who've done these things, women who would inspire us? We need role models but where are they? Whatever we decide to do and whenever or wherever we decide to do it, it should be our decision to make, but wouldn't it be bloody marvellous to know how someone did what they did and what they were thinking when that life-changing opportunity presented itself?

I want my life beyond 50 to be an enthusiastic life crammed with ambition, hopes and aspirations. I want Life (with a capital 'L') but it won't come to me – I have to go out and hunt it down. I've got to grab it by the throat, beat it into submission and make it into something that fits *me*. I've already decided what I will put up with and what I won't. And that brings me to why I wrote this book.

Last year, I decided I was going to write something useful about middle age – to take a look at what happens to us, why it happens and what, if anything, we can do about it, which bits we accept and which bits we make a bit of bother about. From midlife crises and whether they exist to brain fade and invisibility; from enduring the 'little griefs' when everything starts to head south to how attitudes in the media and marketing affect perceptions of age; and to look at the things we're afraid of.

I want to prod my inspiring and gutsy, funny and opinion-ated, waspish and resilient generation into making a noise, into demanding the respect, dignity and rights that we've earned and deserve. I want to make those grey bits of the 'life map' *our* bits, and as interesting to drive as B-roads often are with all their ups and downs and twisty corners. I want us to know how to look after our own bodywork and how to tune our own engines to sing like an Austin Healey 3000 at full throttle. I want us to make the most almighty fuss and reinvent middle age for the next generation.

That my own life should take an unexpected detour along a cliff edge while I was working on this book made the act of writing it extremely difficult but I don't think I would have understood anything nearly so well as I do now if I hadn't been peering over the precipice.

I
Little griefs

*'Maybe it's true that life begins at
fifty. But everything else starts to wear
out, fall out, or spread out.'*
—PHYLLIS DILLER

Age, the traitor, crept up on me. For a very long time
it seemed as though nothing changed and I might
remain in my heyday forever after all, but then, quite suddenly, things began to creak and fall apart, like kitchen
appliances before Christmas. Which bits of me had been
physically where became more of an abstract memory; as
did their size, shape and the existence of clothes that fitted
properly. In some ways it was easier for me, as a woman, to
acknowledge the onset of natural decay and disintegration
because biology conveniently provided a few helpful mark-
ers, largely arranged around the business of procreation
and therefore largely to do with hormones. Men – and I
think most women think this – seem to get off quite lightly
with a smattering of relatively minor stuff. Hormones play
their part here too, but the general perception remains
that men improve with age while women start to crumple

up like Dracula on a sunny spring day. For the most part men seem to weather the years in a pleasantly worn and crinkly way, like a comfortable old sweater, but whatever happens to the exterior there is still the younger man, just there, twinkling away behind the eyes.

Traces of a younger self still reside in every middle-aged person, of course. I remember how my nan used to tap her forehead and say 'I'm still eighteen in here'. I have a theory that most of us, men and women, arrest our emotional development, not at eighteen, but some-where in our 30s. As Rolling Stone Keith Richards (69 and looking 89, God love him) said, 'How could it be our 50th anniversary? I'm only 38.' Personally, I thought I was 31 until I was about 46. When I was 31 I was a tiny elfin blonde in a pink lamé dress. It is an image preserved in a photograph and it was the time when I perhaps liked myself best, physically. In all other respects I was an idiot.

It just never occurred to the Younger Me that one day she'd be 59 but there it is, in black and white, on her – on *my* – birth certificate. Undeniably there is more of my life behind than before me. There are the little ageist prompts my body delivers daily with a soft brush of sadness, an irritating reminder that once upon a time I got out of bed in the morning without producing a concerto of squeaks, creaks and groans. I remember being able to sit up in bed (without using my elbows), stretch (without locking my back) and face the world with a dazzling smile. Happily the smile is still there – when I do eventually smile (though I am not, and never have been, what you might call 'a morning person') – that much hasn't changed.

To be honest, I took all that rude good health for granted. I recall an effervescent feeling of energy and enthusiasm in the same way I remember snowy winters and endless perfect summers.

There are not many days that pass without a few tangible reminders that *tempus* is *fugiting*, and much faster than I would like. These reminders add up to little chapters of mild distress that I am ageing and the fact that I really *am* 59 has become impossible to ignore, although it seems equally impossible to accept. The Younger Me in my head and in old photographs starts to show signs of separation anxiety even before we – I – have got out of bed in the morning; but then that Younger Me usually got a better night's sleep than the older me does. It's not a great way to start the day and it's only one of a growing catalogue of small sorrows and minor niggles that plague me on a regular basis and at different hours of the day and night. For a start, I'm not always entirely sure when my day begins any more but perhaps you'll understand what I mean if we take a gentle canter through what might be a typical day; we'll begin, as I often do, in the middle of the night.

SLEEP

The Younger Me used to go out like a light as soon as her head hit the pillow and stay like that for a good seven or eight hours. Sadly, this is no longer true. I wouldn't stake a fiver on a whole undisturbed night's sleep these days. A bit like playing roulette, there is no logic to a win.

So I go to bed simply because I love my bedroom, my bed and a good book. (A psychiatrist would probably tell me I have a womb fixation.) I'll bust a gut to get on a late train home from the other end of the country just to sleep in my own beloved bed, but my bed isn't always my friend. I bought a feather topper because an over-firm mattress and imminent rain sets off a ripple of sciatica. I invested in an expensive, warm-in-winter-cool-in-summer duvet. My sheets are nubbly, soft French linen. I've taken a lot of time and trouble over creating a cosy cocoon in which sleep will happen. And it does, for the first three or four hours, but then I'll be screwing my eyes shut against the three o'clock wee.

The three o'clock wee isn't always driven by a genuine need to wee but by the time I've convinced myself that I don't need to wee I'm awake and worrying that I need a pre-emptive wee anyway. Also known as the 'investment wee', this is the wee you have even though you may not necessarily want to because it saves you having to wee later, at a less opportune moment. So (eyes opened as little as possible) I fumble my way to the bathroom before return-ing to bed, where, with an infuriating sense of entitlement, the cat's now occupying the lovely warm hollow I left two minutes earlier. I am, of course, thoroughly awake. So I eject the cat and read until I nod off and my book smacks me in the face, waking me up to begin the whole wretched business all over again.

I know this three o'clock waking has somehow become a habit but it's one I don't seem able to break and lately I find it coincides with the kind of drenching sweat you should only see on a Grand National winner. Nobody warned me about this. I naively thought a hysterectomy and HRT would spare me much of the horror of the menopause (at least that's what my consultant told me) but oh no. Now I find it's caught up with me just the same. There is nothing to be done when you wake up in a bed mysteriously transformed into a Turkish bath – or rather, there is: you have to get up and change the sheets, pyjamas, everything, otherwise your bedroom takes on that peculiar musty scent indicative of a resident adolescent. The worst thing is the anticipation. The anticipation of it sometimes wakes me up and I feel it starting. It's not dissimilar to an efficient central heating boiler – it fires up silently somewhere around my middle and in a matter of seconds everything is aglow but at least that has the advantage of allowing some precautionary shedding of bedclothes, so not all night time waking is bad.

But then there are the Technicolour nightmares, which *are* bad and arrive in a chicken-and-egg partnership with the sweats. And there's having one ear cocked for someone trying to nick the car. There's being asleep yet not asleep, while a parade of passing night-distorted worries nip and pinch so that every time I feel myself slipping drowsily into the arms of Morpheus I jerk back up again in alarm. There's the recurring 'zombie dream': will the bolt on the front door hold, is the cat safe, do I have enough food in …? None of this nonsense ever kept Younger Me awake.

I had hoped that having arrived at a time of relative peace in my life and not, for example, having one eye on the clock waiting for teenagers to arrive home 'quietly' at 2.00am would mean I'd sleep the deep and satisfying sleep of the untroubled. Not so. In the absence of more mundane things to worry about my brain is in overdrive, busily inventing ever more fantastical reasons to be awake – the other night I dreamt I was making Brian May and a badger a mug of Bovril. I ask you, what hope is there?

Although, at least I have the comfort of knowing I'm not alone in the wee small hours; if I drop in on Twitter it seems that half the middle-aged population of the UK fix a baleful eye on the alarm clock and tune in to the World Service at around 3.00am. If we're not waking ourselves up with our own snoring, we're grinding our teeth; if we're not mentally running through the soundtrack to *West Side Story*, we're worrying about whether we remembered to worry about renewing the car insurance; and if we're not engaged in a subconscious mental workout there will be the twinges and tics, and aches and pains, that suddenly start up because there is no better time to transmit distress signals than the dead of night. They don't call 3.00am 'the Devil's hour' for nothing.

I took a sleeping pill once – never again. Medicated sleep is as akin to proper rest as a jar of mayonnaise is to a hat. I spent roughly eighteen hours in a sponge-like state with barely enough functioning neurons to make a cup of tea. Was I awake? I don't know.

Still, as long as there remains a chance of fitting in a Second Sleep it is possible to survive. Second Sleep is the silver lining to the insomniac's dark cloud, and means waking early enough to take breakfast back to bed before snatching maybe an hour's worth of delicious snooze. Second Sleep is blissful but be warned, it's also highly addictive and becomes an essential part of your routine before you can count 20 sheep. A surfeit of Second Sleep leads only to more sleeplessness, night reading and lying awake worrying about whether your irregular sleep patterns will lead to early onset dementia. It's a somnambulist's high-wire balancing act: on the one hand I can doze off for ten minutes almost anywhere, while on the other, eight hours' restorative slumber routinely proves beyond me.

Oh to wake joyfully to the sound of birdsong and church bells, with pale rays of early morning sun gently illuminating a face free of pillow creases and refreshed by a splendid night's sleep. Fat chance. Instead I am condemned to surface groggily from beneath the duvet, having spent a good portion of the night engaged in more nocturnal activity than the average bat. Please let me sleep and I promise I will *never* take it for granted again.

FACING THE WORLD

There are two sides to this business of ageing – the psychological side and the physical side – and they craftily embrace during the fraught process of getting proper clothes on in the morning and preparing to face the world. This is a routine I used to enjoy, and yet the older I become the more I feel deeply and symbiotically attached to my pyjamas. Mostly I try to avoid looking at myself in the mirror until I'm properly dressed. Silly, isn't it? I blame the Younger Me in that damned photograph for causing a reaction of mild shock should I catch sight of my 59-year-old reflection. I'm not so hung up that I chew my nails to bits every morning in a frenzy of self-loathing, because I do, on the whole, quite like myself and think that I'm doing all right, but what's there on the outside is at odds with how I imagine myself on the inside. I look at pictures of Younger Me in nineteen eighty-something and see a pretty young woman who I recall never believed she *was* pretty. That's something I hear a lot from women of my generation. I wonder sometimes whether it would have made any difference to the decisions she made if she'd known it. I feel sad that she didn't know it. But to keep trying to second-guess such things is pointless and depressing … that way madness lies. It's best to just let it go and smile at the silliness of her and at all the thought-less fun she had, because once she was me, and somewhere inside myself I am still her.

Anyway, I digress. But it seems to me that it's becoming almost impossible to balance these two selves, dress appropriately (whatever *that* is), and leave the house looking halfway decent. Observing how other women do it I've noticed that quite a few my age adopt a sort of uniform. It's usually trouser-based with a loose top or shirt and never, on any account, do these women tuck something into a waistband. By and large they are right. Waistbands in particular are the enemy of the middle-aged. As a middle-aged woman it can be hard to know where one's waist is. Even if you're stick-thin your waist will have migrated. I took my eye off my waist for a couple of months when I was 45 and it moved. It's what they do.

Knees undergo a similar metamorphosis. I grieve for the smooth knees of my youth: firm knees, knees that I could kneel on, silent knees, knees that made it possible to wear a chic hemline with bare legs. Or shorts. God, I miss shorts and by that I mean proper shorts, not the mid-length variety that are usually teamed with a sun visor and a bum bag. Living my life energetically via the mediums of dancing, riding and childrearing has rendered my knees unsuitable for polite company. Dancing and riding both employ knees in major ways and, inconveniently, in different directions: ballet dictates the knees are turned *out* while riding demands they are turned *in*. Thanks in no small part to this I now have only semi-functional knees, and semi-functional knees are, I suspect, largely responsible for my falling off a kerb in Kensington High Street, in broad daylight, without having touched anything stronger than a chai latte. Falling off a kerb at 51 – the shame! – damaged my dignity, my left knee and frightened a taxi driver half to death.

Fortunately, internal knee wear is invisible to the casual observer (unless unintentionally revealed by slow and awkward rising from the kneeling or seated position gripping tightly to any conveniently located weight-bearing structure) but one of the most significant ageing benchmarks, the wrinkled knee, is not. Are any of us prepared for the shock of the wrinkled knee? I know the Younger Me was not. Wrinkled knees are, after all, the clear outward sign that one's skin is losing its youthful elasticity, like a puckered, deflating balloon. I regard my own battered knees with a mournful sadness and think 'thank heaven for

100 denier black opaque tights'. With black opaque tights the on-the-knee dress is again an option during autumn and winter, and possibly a little bit of spring. Perhaps even up until the end of April, which is a good seven months' worth all told. Hallelujah.

These days deciding what to wear is a right old faff but often a great deal easier than actually putting the stuff on; just try putting on socks or tights when you have sciatica, or fastening a bra when you have a frozen shoulder. For an entire year I was condemned to wear only one particular tartan frock because a frozen shoulder meant I couldn't zip anything else up and pride wouldn't allow me to ask a colleague to do it after I'd arrived at work because that would have felt like the Beginning of the End. I endured sixteen months of agony and physiotherapy to get my shoulder working again, only to be told that frozen shoulders often happen randomly at my age and will eventually put themselves right after about eighteen months. If I'd known that I could have saved myself no end of bother.

Back in the days when I could look good in almost anything (Younger Me again) getting dressed and deciding which character I would be today was a pleasure. Now it's almost too hard – a tough NATO-like negotiation involving tactical manoeuvring and a compromise before I can get started on everything else. I find it a struggle to decide which of my ageing bits and pieces are the more socially acceptable (and therefore merit exposure) and which might require a quick scrutiny of the *Daily Mail* 'Sidebar of Shame' to verify that fact. Do I want to be visible or would I rather fade into the background? Why is it apparently beyond the wit of man and fashion designers to create clothes for women with more than half a metre of fabric between neckline and hemline? Or that look good on someone other than a fourteen-year-old giraffe?

If I can fudge something together from my wardrobe, there can be no such obfuscation where my face is concerned. Everyone looks at everyone else's face and everyone notices the smallest mistake, except me and perhaps other women in their middle years who find their eyesight is thankfully less efficient. I like make-up. I like eyeliner and scarlet lipstick. However it's becoming increasingly difficult to get everything in the right place and then persuade it to stay there rather than wandering off around my face before an important meeting. No one used to worry too much about this in the '70s but now apparently we must look box fresh and photo ready at every minute of the day. Not that it matters too much for we invisible women because it seems no one wants to take our photographs anyway, least of all us. Which sort of makes it all right not to worry, I suppose; only I do … I do.

There are vexing decisions to be made every day before I finally recognise what I've known all along: that no one except me gives a damn anyway. I have missed *many* trains because of this.

Commuting and work

Why can't I sit down on a train instead of standing, wedged under someone's armpit, while someone else uses my head as a bookrest? When I first moved to London I enjoyed it. I honestly, truly did. I think it was the novelty of playing sardines with a bunch of total strangers every day. The Younger Me was pretending to be Carrie from *Sex and the City*, cosmopolitan, self-possessed and (mostly) having fun. Inevitably, the fantasy has paled. Commuting in London is purgatory. The escalators! The crush! The route march between the Northern and Central lines when your feet are blistered and your sling-back's snapped. The endless, bloody signal failures ... I'm too old for this. If I'm lucky enough to get a seat it's the one squashed between someone eating pickled onion Monster Munch and someone else with an indecently loud MP3 player and rubbish head-phones. If I'm offered a seat I gratefully accept and post up a little prayer to the all-seeing God of Commuters asking him not to whisk me off to the Dungeon of the Weak for being too old and feeble to keep up with the rest of the stampeding herd. I rage inwardly when sharp-elbowed City boys hustle on to the train the very second the doors start to open and grab whatever space there is. I suppose what I'm missing is old-fashioned good manners, which immediately identifies me to other middle-aged persons as a fellow sufferer.

It seems to me there are only so many years you can do the work thing before you begin to feel as though you're stuck in Groundhog Day; at least, that's my theory. It doesn't matter how much I loved what I did at any par-ticular time, there was always a point at which I'd start to feel a little jaded, a little weary of it all, and what oppor-tunities there were didn't thrill me quite as much as they used to. And it takes so much *energy*. In my middle age an intense 50- or 60-hour week (not including a social life) can have me arriving at the weekend feeling as though I've had a stroke. Once upon a time Younger Me would take it all in her stride and was even known on occasion to turn up at work in whatever she was wearing when she went out the night before (in the 1970s this was regarded as a magnificent achievement and not the Walk of Shame it is now). The faint shock I feel at recognising I lack much of the stamina I once had is, I'm afraid, another symptom of my 59 years on planet Earth.

Over time, as fate and circumstance propelled my life along its course, I'd adapted from accommodating the demands of college and a social life to the needs of work, a husband and children, and I was very busy. When life demanded I adapt myself to working and children with no husband, I was busier still. Yet further down the line my routine eventually became focused on accommodating just my job and me, which strangely made me even busier ... but the fact is, although I'd always claimed never to have suffered from 'empty nest' syndrome, when I started to put work before everything else that is *exactly* what I was suffering from. Most of my life had been about putting family and other people and things first. When my family grew up a career took its place. It is, of course, a displacement activity of sorts. Work became something I rigorously exploited as a reason not to address the issues I should have been addressing – such as a vague underlying sadness and the nagging sense that something somewhere had come adrift. It had. I had. For years I'd resolutely ignored the physical and psychological effects of growing older and in that denial I'd built myself a lifestyle that far exceeded my middle-aged resources. Put simply I wore myself out.

One of the biggest problems with my accrued personal energy deficit is that it leaves me with little inclination to pop out of the office at lunchtime for a little cheerer-upper in the form of some light but self-indulgent retail therapy. Wherever I've worked there were nearly always *shops* and in London the shops are fairy palaces of instant gratification. And that can cause problems of another sort.

SHOPPING AND BODY IMAGE

Time was when office lunchtimes meant slipping out to hunt for something frothy and delicious to wear on the coming Saturday night (I'd like to pause here for a brief moment while I gaze into the middle distance and retrieve some fond memories of Younger Me, nightclubs and my lost collection of Biba frocks ...). Middle age, alas, is much more likely to find me hunting the length of Oxford Street on a quest for that Holy Grail of Corsetry: the perfect bra. Without the perfect bra it is pointless buying anything else because nothing will look right or hang right. This is also when I will appreciate that the light in my bedroom is an awful lot kinder to my anatomy than the lights in any department store fitting room where I look like an especially well-nourished cadaver in a pathology lab. I had no idea that cellulite could cover a whole body; when I get under those lights I swear even my ear lobes have cellulite.

Buying properly fitting underwear in your 50s is an ordeal and I do so wish it wasn't because underwear – but do let's call it lingerie – is infinitely pleasing and I enjoy nothing better than a languorous excursion through Selfridge's knicker department. However, one is very much afraid that one's 'smalls' are no longer small, or certainly not as small as they used to be. I am well aware of this. I do not need to be reminded. But leave me with my vision of frilly knick-knacks, because I am deeply sad about the loss of one of life's great pleasures. Lingerie for the middle-aged woman would not look out of place in Wagner's Ring Cycle and it's not fair. I want it at least to be pretty if it can no longer be insubstantial and if the eternal problem of fitting room lights and shoddy service could be resolved once and for all there would be an enormous 'BOOM!' as grey pound spending shot through the sound barrier. I wouldn't mind being deceived by clever lighting – I'd love it. I want lace. I want silk. I want scanty(ish) scanties for the middle-aged. And when the time comes I want to be tucked into my coffin in a full set of Agent Provocateur. With big knickers.

Of course, the problem principally arises from my ever-changing body shape and in particular, the bits that have blighted my whole life with their reluctance to find a shape they like and settle down. I'm talking about breasts, and I don't think I'm unusual in having a less than straight-forward relationship with mine. I spent a lot of time when I was about twelve longing for a pair of proper grown-up ones and then when I got them I wished they'd go away again. To be honest, they weren't much practical use and they were a source of permanent blush-making embarrassment, what with the jiggling inappropriateness of them. I can't look at a Galia without remembering my nickname at school (I struggled beneath the 'Melons' moniker all through Grammar).

In the 1960s we had Playtex 'Cross your Heart' and while I might have yearned for something a tiny bit sophisticated and grown up, what I actually got was a couple of pink nylon pointy things strapped to my chest. I hated them and most of all I hated that I didn't reach the ends (I don't think anyone did). As a result I spent my days permanently looking down, not through modesty or shyness but on constant lookout for a dented bosom. Once I got fully fired up with teenage rebelliousness I went out and bought myself a bright yellow Mary Quant Booby Trap, which was basically a pair of tights made into a bra. But of course that was then, when my breasts more or less supported themselves – by the time I was 23 and pregnant with my first daughter they'd begun a determined bid for an independent life of their own.

Over the next five years my boobage went from 32A to 36G three times and never quite returned to its pert, pre-childbearing loveliness. The weight of fully functioning baby-feeding breasts connived with gravity to drop my rack down my sternum by a good three ribs' worth – standing up, that is. If I lay down they'd slide off sideways into my armpits. Catherine Deneuve is credited with saying 'at a certain age you have to choose between your face and your ass'. I respectfully suggest that Catherine Deneuve may have been wrong. The choice is, in fact, between your face and your boobs, or maybe your face, your boobs AND your ass. But then you see, your 'ass' also forms an unholy alliance with the bastard gravity and disappears. It's true! I don't know where it goes, but the luscious assembly of *gluteus maximus* that helped Younger Me look so utterly fabulous in a bikini doesn't any more, simply because *it's not there* (and I'm 59 and not *her* any more). I assume it has something to do with all the sitting. In any life there is a great deal of sitting but if you work in an office (or make your living as a writer) there's even more sitting. My *derrière*, sadly, is now flat and another source of woe. However, I do hear that someone has invented 'bum bras'. Incredible.

Weirdly, struggling through my sixth decade, I find there's been a slight bosom reversal. As the rest of me surrenders to the fickleness of hormones, gravitational pull, food cravings and the passage of time, my boobs are enjoying something of a renaissance, having taken on a more matronly aspect. It's peculiar but I do feel I'm warming to them again ... apart from the forked cleavage, which I loathe.

The forked or multiple cleavage, looking like an aerial view of the Mississippi delta, seems to be mostly caused by overenthusiastic application of tight corsetry (the mono-bosom) and an excess of sunbathing. Yes, it makes sense to address the gravitational issue with serious scaffolding, but on the other hand the more bra straps are shortened the more ... spillage there is. If there's one thing middle-aged flesh does not take kindly to, it's being constrained – why else the elasticated waistband?

If I hoick my bra straps too far, or fasten the back a notch too snugly, my body will wrestle to be free – witness the peculiar 'four-breasted effect' usually seen in partnership with the 'back-fat muffin top'. In fact, muffin tops are yet another example of resistance work by the body's covert operations unit – it doesn't matter whether you're thin or fat, somewhere about your person there will be a muffin top struggling to get out, and you will know it is. Maybe I'll add muffin tops to my sleepless worry list.

The upshot of all this is that lunchtime isn't nearly long enough to try on bras properly (and discover in the process that cost bears no relationship to fit). It will always end with a frenetic dash back to the office, late, sweaty and breathless, having bought nothing at all, not even a sandwich.

PARTYING FOR THE OVER-50S

Of course, if there is a light at the end of the (nap-less) afternoon office tunnel then it's the likelihood that there will be a party somewhere, or dinner with friends or, at the very least, drinks with colleagues. Work brings new people into your life and, along with that, some degree of socialising. Or it would if I hadn't perforated my eardrum a couple of years ago. Now, while I can see *when* someone is talking to me, I can't always hear *what* they're saying, which means I can't really reply either without sounding like an idiot. I can smile and nod as though I understand every word but sooner or later someone will ask me what I think of UKIP and I'll reply, 'They're all right if you like that sort of thing – except for all the bones, of course.'

If it's not my ears then it's my mouth saying something it shouldn't, like 'prophylactic' instead of 'anaphylactic'. I expect there's been a short circuit somewhere, probably something to do with the effect of alcohol on my ageing metabolism. Consequently – and because I've lost the ability to hear and speak properly in civilised company – large gatherings have become social minefields, although, happily, I do find that the (several) drink(s) that might possibly have caused the problem in the first place also help enormously with any subsequent embarrassment. The Younger Me would have approved of that. On the other hand, she wouldn't like the fact that something very peculiar has happened to her alcohol tolerance in middle age and she will never be quite sure how it's going to take her.

There's nothing wrong with a whiff of unpredictability to an evening out and many a glorious adventure can materialise as a result. But I'm far less enthused by this strange hinterland where I'm either a total lightweight or knocking them back at a rate of knots while still coherently discussing the plays of Harold Pinter or Dali's influence on the YBAs. My alcohol tolerance in my 50s is all over the place and I cannot make sense of it. It is a source of sorrow and occasional shame that I, who was once introduced by a lawyer not usually known for his sobriety as 'the only woman who can drink me under the table', should find myself intermittently kiboshed by two tiny plastic cups of cat's piss Chardonnay. Where there used to be a predetermined formula to work by – estimated length of evening + food = optimum intake of alcohol per hour (more or less) – there is now no predictable pattern. Sharing a bottle of Gavi over lunch with a friend is fine. Six Mojitos and a solitary canapé is obviously *not* fine, although the last time I tried it I was still able to stand, walk and speak but mysteriously unable to write. A modest glass of Chablis at my desk of an evening might be all right but there again it might not and I'll find I can't pronounce the word 'editor', which is unfortunate when I work in an editor's office. On the other hand, a stupid quantity of house plonk together with three crisps, a single peanut and a shared bag of pork scratchings, then rolling home at five in the morning doesn't seem to present any serious problems. So that blows the 'pace yourself' theory out of the water.

Over the course of a few years working for the *Guardian* newspaper the Edinburgh Festival became one of my favourite August fixtures – three days of culture and heroic partying with prodigious quantities of alcohol and very little sleep. It was bloody fantastic. But it takes stamina to stack up a lunch, a reception, a dinner and a late soirée, roll into bed at 3.00am and then roll out again four hours later for a full Scottish breakfast before skipping off to an early morning contemporary dance performance – stamina, intermittent bacon sandwiches, coffee and those fizzy vitamin tablets. I could do all that and still look reasonably fresh-faced and bushy-tailed. Not any more, I can't. And as if that isn't enough, I find my brain and body provide me with far less warning than they used to of when I'm approaching 'critical mass' – that being the point at which the Inner Voice of Reason announces to the sensible grown-up part of my brain that it's time to put the glass down and drink water for a while. My Inner Voice of Reason and my brain have altogether ceased effective dialogue where alcohol is concerned and flicker on and off like a pair of defective light bulbs. Lately my dysfunctional (and frankly deluded) Inner Voice has been responsible for one or two awkward cock-ups by going off a bit late, and it's never a good thing to see a middle-aged woman attempting a discreet exit on all fours. I suppose what this demonstrates is that a late-developing sense of responsibility is replacing Younger Me's reckless and joyful pissed-ness.

To occasionally get thoroughly and hysterically bladdered with friends is one of life's great pleasures but it seems my days of such high jinks as dancing barefoot around a policeman in the rain and holding the pub dog to ransom are behind me. Have I, at last, and with a good deal of regret, finally grown up? And don't grown-ups go home at a sensible hour ...? Well, stuff that.

HOME ALONE

One of the main things expected of you as a grown-up is that you will get married, or at least cohabit, and perhaps have children. And I did do this. I did it because I wanted to – or thought I did – and I did it for a whole fifteen years. I have three amazing daughters and a whole tribe of gorgeous grandchildren to show for it, and I shouldn't feel sad about this but I do. It's a tugging sort of sadness that quietly waits for me to drop my guard, usually when I'm about to go to a party on my own, or perhaps first thing in the morning (often, awkwardly, when I'm staying away somewhere), and then there's a sudden surge of alone-ness and my eyes fill up.

I don't mind being alone. I enjoy the selfishness of it and the peace, and it's true that 'alone' is not the same as 'lonely'. All the same, I feel the loss of my sweet, funny little girls, who are now grown-ups themselves, and occasionally I feel it very acutely. What I'm feeling, I suppose, is nostalgia. I miss the more certain time when I was sure of my role in life, whereas now I am a middle-aged single woman adrift in a world that doesn't know what to do with her. I have to remind myself that this life without ties can be whatever I want it to be. I have to remind myself of what I want and what makes me happy.

Motherhood is only part of who I am but it is a big part and it's hard to put your heart and soul into nurturing something and then let it go. It seems to me there's a kind of inevitable fracture in life that happens around middle age and how you mend it and get on with the next stage is hugely important because the next stage is mostly about *you* and sometimes that means going out and finding your 'couple' life again and sometimes it means learning to be happy on your own.

I don't understand why so many people believe the only route to happiness is to be *with* someone. Why do so many women of my age move heaven, earth and Internet dating websites to find their next care project? Personally, I'm not really fussed about entering that particular market again and it seems that the only time my life derails is when I'm persuaded to do something about it, usually against my better judgement. Younger Me would not have understood this attitude at all.

It seems to me there is a deep divide between those people who have never learned to be on their own, who are frightened by the prospect of an empty house, who devote a great deal of money, time, energy and personal sacrifice to continually searching for 'the one', and those others who would rather not go through all that again unless someone can deliver up Mr or Mrs Right with the minimum of fuss and bother. Personally I agree with whoever said that it's better to be alone than to be with the wrong person. I love men. I do. I'm just not sure I want one under my feet or in my bathroom.

It also seems to me that at some point in anyone's life there is a reasonable chance they will find themselves on their own, whether by choice or not. Being alone is an essential life skill – we must learn the knack and get on with it so we're prepared and not afraid when our turn comes around. To be honest, I can think of few things more satisfying than waking on a Saturday morning and asking myself what I'd like to do today; being able to answer 'Anything you like, Walmers' is a pleasure I would find hard to let go.

Very occasionally, when I succumb to a singleton's worries about dying alone and being eaten by cats, I browse a dating website or two. I find I have a tolerance of roughly fifteen minutes. Men my own age are looking at 30- to 40-year-olds and men who are older than me seem to make themselves deliberately unappealing, although they are well balanced by that chip on each shoulder. I calculate that the happy hunting ground for your average 59-year-old woman is marginally below the 80-year mark. And indeed it's true that I appear to be total catnip to octogenarians, which is a bit depressing, although often amusing, and frequently presents unexpected hazards in my social life.

As a result I've convinced myself that I'm past it. But then I clap eyes on Daniel Craig or Bill Nighy and know that should the opportunity ever arise for either of them to chase me around the furniture, I wouldn't run very fast. I probably wouldn't run at all. However, until then I'm stuck with the responsibility of getting myself into a taxi at the end of a night out, picking up a pint of milk from the garage on the way home and appeasing a couple of loftily disinterested cats occupying the moral high ground because their supper's late. The odd thing is that I like it that way. I like it a lot.

Age before bedtime

In all this mountain of quandary and Younger Me-inspired daily torment, there is one other thing that I can't work out at all, or rather I can but I don't like to admit to it: why does the sight of the young and carefree provoke a funny feeling around my heart and an urgent need to weep gently into my coffee? I've been feeling that for a while, I just wasn't sure what it was – I thought it was hormones or panic. Now I know it's a mixture of all sorts of things, including happiness, regret, envy and wonderment. The young take their youth so much for granted and, bless them, they don't know what they've got. They can't imagine a time when they won't have it or when they'll be grateful they used to have it because others in their heat of life's race didn't pass the 100-metre flag. No wonder I'm surprised by photographs of a Younger Me – I'm still here after all, at an age I couldn't imagine myself being when I was 30. I can uselessly speculate that perhaps I should have been less susceptible to flattery, less eager to please or less willing to put up with the unacceptable because it was the only thing I knew … but in that not-so-distant past, what a girl looked like was almost more important than anything else so I used what I had to get me where I wanted to be and that's why it's so hard to let go.

Now, at a time when we should be feeling more comfortable and confident in our own skin, what seems to matter most is not how pretty we are but how *young* we look, prettiness can be added later. Like icing a plain and ordinary cake, we can have every crevice filled, frozen and lifted. We can have our eyelashes extended, our brows tattooed, our lips permanently lipsticked, our hair lengthened, shortened or augmented. We can look as weird, surprised and stretched as we like just as long as we continue 'young'. I had the perfect opportunity to study one of the most remarked upon and admired facelifts of the last decade when I found myself in a restaurant at the table next to the woman who'd had it done, and it *was* remarkable. Or it was until she stood up to leave the room – because there is no surgery (at the moment) to make you move like the 30-year-old you're pretending to be. Her posture and movement revealed her as the 66-year-old she was.

All this expensive self-delusion is tied up with our apparent inability to accept ourselves as we age, although there is some hope because we *are* beginning to get better at it. However, still, the fear I hear expressed most often is 'what will happen to me when I lose my looks?' Half of us are worried about what's coming (or going) while the other half have experienced it already and had their worst fears confirmed, apparently. But who says it has to be a bad thing? The more we worry, the more it becomes a self-fulfilling prophecy. The more we worry, the more we erode our confidence and self-esteem; and the more we do this, the more we fade from public view because we accept a biased and arbitrary judgement about our physical currency once we pass 50. And so it continues. But now more than ever, it's the person *inside* who's important and becomes more so as time passes. Whatever magazines, films, advertisers and the media preach at us about doing all we can and more to maintain an increasingly generic 'beauty' (doesn't everyone look more or less the same when they're 'enhanced'?) it is always that unique inner person who makes us who we are, even as the outside gets crow's feet, uneven eyebrows and age spots.

Of course it would be easier just to wrap yourself in a duvet with a bottle of gin and ignore everything. Yes, let's not go out because the public must be protected against the sight of older women; let's keep quiet about the many injustices we suffer simply because we choose not to nip, tuck, lift and inject; let's accept our exclusion from the fashion world and be grateful for whatever beige tent we're offered as consolation; and yes, let's ignore ageism in all its incarnations and not speak out because someone just might be rude to us. When I was 56 I had a period of about eighteen months where I struggled to get myself out of bed, never mind out of the door. Everything was too much effort. I think I had recognised, and was adjusting to, the loss of who I had been, the Younger Me who relished opportunities and challenges, who rolled about in life like a seal on a sandbar. Then there came a spell when I had an internal debate with myself before every trip to the theatre or to a party, or coffee with friends or going out for a walk. I questioned everything. It was exhausting but it was part of learning to stand strong and alone, to walk into a room full of people on my own, to speak to people I'd never met as well as those I knew well, to be independent and to build a new life for myself outside of work and, of course, as an older woman.

Unconsciously I was marking out the boundaries for the next stage of my life and it was hard because it involved a certain amount of risk and a huge amount of nerve. I'd been hit by a number of potential disasters and I was feeling pretty shaky anyway so it took courage I didn't feel I had but I had to take it on or go under. I'd been 'under' and I didn't want to be there again. I am where I am now because of, and in spite of, the successes and mistakes made by the tiny blonde girl who cocked things up but somehow worked it out. If I look at the tools life has given me, and at the things that have already changed and I've hardly noticed, then what's so bad about changing a few more things to make it all even better, to make my life suit *me*?

The last two years have been, as a documentary might say, 'an interesting journey'. If I'd known what I was letting myself in for I'm not sure I'd have bought the ticket, but I did buy it, and because I did I know that I have moved on from feeling all those little griefs for the me that was. I have mourned her too long. She will always be there because she is in me, with me, and at the heart of the woman I have become. We've got through all that life has thrown at us to arrive here together, to stand on the threshold of even greater adventures, both of us survivors. The Younger Me lives on, just in slightly different packaging.

2

Reasoning backwards

> *'In solving a problem of this sort, the grand
> thing is to be able to reason backwards ... a
> very useful accomplishment, and a very easy
> one, but people do not practise it much'*
> —Sherlock Holmes

The above quote does not, of course, refer to the great sleuth's thoughts on middle age but instead begins a short passage on the process of deductive reasoning. When I read it I was struck by how it seemed to offer me a means of working out not only how I arrived here and why I'm the way I am now that I have, but also how to make sense of life and live it properly, in hope. Middle age is quite simply another part of life, one that we all go through if we're lucky. It's true that reaching 50 requires a certain amount of adjustment and reflection, and mainly because in these unenlightened times middle age is mostly seen as an undesirable, problematic few years for a woman but it's vital we change this and see it as an opportunity for flowering and growth, rather than as a time for the mothballing of hopes and dreams. Middle age is not the problem – how we think about it is.

Whatever your personal circumstances, what turning 50 should really be like is being given a passport to freedom, choice and opportunity. It can be that – I know, I've been there. But I keep slipping back, because once you break away from the pre-ordained middle age model, it proves a little difficult to hold on to the mindset that set you free; to keep up the optimism, guts and drive. It's not easy and you might not think you have the stomach for any more struggles but your sixth decade could, and should, be anything and everything you want it to be – if you choose to see it that way. Or you could just swallow the media message that we should 'fight' age, treat it like a disease or disability and approach it like a mongoose tackles a snake.

If, as Sherlock Holmes says, we are to reason backwards, a lot can be solved by what went before. The past is where future answers lie. We each have pasts where we made mistakes, surrendered when we should have battled, made a hideous awful mess of things but picked ourselves up and soldiered on because … well, what other choice did we have? Did we accept everything we were told in our teens or twenties or did we question it and go all out to build our own lives? It's only by looking back that we can move forward.

Despite the rise, fall and rise again of feminism, life for women continues to be largely bound up in our ability to attract, reproduce, empower, support and nurture others so that when we're faced with a spell in life when we can finally get on with doing things for our own selves we find it hard to be as thrilled as we should be – the most we can manage is a kind of non-committal shrug. We're tired. We haven't thought about it. We're not sure what to do about middle age or with it, or what it's for, exactly. If having youth is perpetual Christmas then middle age is that weird patch between Boxing Day and New Year's Eve when you don't quite know how to occupy yourself. With old age we sort of know what to expect, more or less, and we do at least see old people doing old people things in films, on TV and in advertising, even if they are mostly ridiculous cartoon stereotypes; middle age we don't see much of at all. We see plenty of old women yet middle-aged women remain largely invisible and I wonder why that is. Is it because we've come to identify middle age with a whiff of staleness? Is it because no one wants to see middle-aged women – not even middle-aged women? Why? It's hard to aspire to something you can't see, to know how to be or behave.

When we're swamped with so much negativity we forget we are still *us* and that we have things to be getting on with – our lives, for example. Has middle age become a state of mind where we, prematurely, start to think in terms of whether the eye-wateringly expensive new coat we have our eye on (indeed can't resist) will outlive us, and whether we'll need to replace the oven/washing machine/bed/saucepans before we drop off the perch or forget what the damn things are for? My brain's been up to this too and in a way it's right, but sitting there in my head predicting my demise, or else conjuring possible futures of such Orwellian bleakness that whenever I think about it I have to breathe into a paper bag, is unhelpful to put it mildly.

It's all bollocks, of course, but at the same time I know I've become painfully aware of my own mortality. Now this is obviously linked to me weathering a couple of years peppered with loss and death but I also think my feelings have a lot to do with suddenly noticing that while I've been faffing about 'fighting' middle age like a good little soldier I've suddenly woken up to the fact that I'm almost 60; in other words I've wasted practically the whole of my own middle age instead of using it to do something, anything, that might helpfully contribute to my 'Third Age'. Now I'm assailed by the same sort of guilt that used to accompany late homework, and obsessed with nit-picking irrelevancies. For instance, I worry about spending an afternoon on the sofa in blissful idleness with a good book because I haven't actually *done* anything. I agonise over what possessed me to put my car keys in the sock drawer and whether this means I'm starting to go doolally tap. Instead of simply changing the light bulb at the top of the stairs (a task I am perfectly capable of) I run through a complicated risk assessment of what could go wrong: temporary dizziness leading to fall/electrocution/eventual death/eaten by the cat? I constantly question what I want and what I need and I am further confused that these are not necessarily the same thing – I can *want* a new pair of shoes but do I actually *need* them? I mean, for the love of Pete, if we're all doing this day in and day out no wonder poor sleep is so endemic in middle age.

There is one thing that helps us out just a little bit and that's the nebulous nature of middle age – it's a small point but it does play to our advantage. I like that no one seems able to decide exactly when it is but we could go on forever with the '50 is the new 40' argument and it's basically nonsense anyway because no, it's not. People do like to label things though so for the sake of argument let's shift the *OED*'s current start date five years forward so that middle age commences at 50. That sounds much more realistic to me. When I was 45 I was dating an Italian man ten years younger than me (most invigorating) but I'd also held my eldest daughter's hand during the birth of my first grandchild – in terms of human behaviour I make this almost middle-aged but not quite. This 'flip-siding' happened a lot in my mid- to late forties and it was a bit like having a foot in both camps. I'd be in the gym at least three times a week sweating and grunting my way to a youthful physique but I remember looking up during a bench press and noticing the inside of my elbow had gone all crinkly. At this stage I would say I was slightly in denial. I kept telling myself it was all going swimmingly but there were faint alarm bells somewhere in my psycho-logical middle distance. I felt as though I was perpetually looking for something I wasn't sure I could find … even if I knew what it was in the first place.

Then disaster struck: I lost my job in the NHS and with that discovered that in terms of new career oppor-tunities I was not so much over the hill as six feet under it, pushing up daisies in the burial ground for middle-aged aspirations that was the Midlands employment market. I lost valuable time job-hunting because I couldn't quite bring myself to believe that where prospective employers were concerned my extensive experience was apparently as current as the crinoline. That they could make that assumption without even meeting me made me want to smash things. They assumed they knew how I looked, how I worked, what my level of ambition was and how I would fit into their company by making a lazy generalisation based on what exactly? It had been a long time since I put my date of birth on my CV but employers work it out. Eventually I took a job, because I had to, on a fraction of my NHS salary, working as a receptionist, building an elastic band ball the size of a watermelon in my lunch breaks. I was bored to tears.

Boredom's always good for a kick in the pants. A couple of months and at least three elastic band balls later I decided this would not be the way I spent what remained of my working life; a bullet would be kinder. With my children grown up, I was to all intents and purposes without ties so I started looking elsewhere, with the intention of relocating and giving myself a completely fresh start. I researched Edinburgh and London, settling on England's capital because it seemed a richer and more accessible source of opportunities (as well as physically nearer), and in a short space of time I had myself registered with three secretarial agencies. My experience counted for something! The relief that provincial ageist attitudes did not extend south of Watford Gap was a total head rush.

Next I had to go there, to London, for interviews. I remember getting off the train at St Pancras: my legs were shaking so badly I could hardly walk. I didn't know London and had no idea what to expect (a mugging probably) but at the time I had the kind of burning conviction that builds empires, and I took the leap. The Italian (now occasional long-distance) boyfriend asked me what I would do if I were offered a job. 'I'll take it of course!' There was doubt in his question; he'd thrown down a gauntlet, not believing I would or could do it. But I did do it, I got myself a job, I found myself a house share in Stratford and moved to London. It was all completely terrifying but by god, it got the career wheels spinning again. Eventually, in 2006 I joined the *Guardian* as personal assistant to the editor-in-chief, by which time I was 51 – firmly middle-aged according to the *OED* (but only just started according to my revised calculation) – and still energetically forward-thinking at an age when everyone assumes middle-aged ladies are happily coasting towards retirement on a gentle tide of G & T, golf clubs and hand-knitted bed socks.

My job at the *Guardian* felt like I'd reached the top of the secretarial tree. It still does; I loved it. Alternately nerve-shredding and unpredictable, or ticking along steadily on the daily rhythm of getting a newspaper out, it would often be both at the same time and it was never less than challenging. Two days were seldom the same. There was a healthy workplace ethos of being encouraged to challenge and question and a good deal of laughter. Everywhere my boss went I went too, two steps behind with a metaphorical dustpan and brush in one hand (there was often a good deal of clearing up required) and a literal bottle of Chablis in the other. My job was to make things happen, smooth things over and organise. I was a fixer and facilitator – I made order out of chaos.

My hours were long and I was on call 24/7 but I loved it passionately until, somewhere around my 57th birthday, I began to wake up on Saturday mornings feeling like a stunned fish. All I wanted to do was stare at the wall, or sleep. I couldn't enjoy a book any more because by the time I'd read one sentence I'd forgotten the one that preceded it. It began to dawn on me that perhaps I wasn't as invincible as I'd thought I was, that my plan to work in this job and, more importantly, at this pace until I retired might not be a runner after all. I hadn't anticipated this: not having the physical strength to keep it up had never occurred to me; burnout wasn't part of my original calculations. There was something else I hadn't prepared for either and if anything it was even more unwelcome: my self-perceived weakness made me feel vulnerable and afraid.

And then, just as I was beginning a contemplation of my own frailty, my father – who every morning and whatever the weather walked at least four miles, who thought nothing of whipping up a new garden shed over a weekend and had lost his voice a month earlier after one of his rare colds – was diagnosed with lung cancer and assigned to palliative care; the tumour was inoperable. Not, I suppose, unexpected for an 85-year-old and yet the news poleaxed me.

At times like this it does feel as though a malign spirit randomly has it in for you but the truth is that it's not an unusual situation for anyone, not in middle age. Still, you never think it will happen to you … until it does. My customary response to one of these perfect storms of catastrophe that land on us every so often ('when sorrows come, they come not single spies but in battalions') is to hang on like grim death to the status quo. As a single mum I would yell, 'Get the wagons in a circle!' if there were problems looming, putting us all on notice to form a tight-knit, mutually supportive family group – a bit like DEFCON 3 but with more tea and chocolate.

When the shit starts to fly I find some sort of displacement activity helpful, so before London, weather permitting, I could be found on the back step holding a one-way conversation with Og the dog and puffing my way through a pack of Marlborough Lights; I kept a box of jumble sale china to throw at the garden wall – a wonderful stress-buster; or I'd make jam, lots and lots of jam ... and pickles ... and chutneys. In London, where I no longer smoke (much), I go and stare meditatively out of a window, or slope off for a coffee somewhere that isn't the office. We all need these head savers. Yes, it's an excuse for not doing things – often for fear of doing the wrong thing – but it's also a way of giving the trammelled brain a pat and a cuddle.

That point, when I was taking emotional hits almost every day and everything I'd built up seemed to be collapsing, was when I started working out what to do next, although on reflection, I was perhaps a bit late getting my arse into gear. Up until 57, when I'd finally achieved the kind of security and status I could only have dreamed of 30 years before, I'd made the very basic error of assuming that because all was hunky dory now it would continue to be so because I Had Arrived; but when it came to it I had no reserves, no Plan B and no thoughts about how I might negotiate my way through this late-life elephant trap. Maintaining the status quo was clearly not an option. I had to make substantial changes. You know those dreams where you're flying but petrified of falling? If I stopped flapping my bingo wings I would certainly fall. How far was anyone's guess. The whole situation was impossible.

> *'You write your life story by the choices you make.*
> *You never know if they have been a mistake.*
> *Those moments of decision are so difficult.'*
> —HELEN MIRREN

It's a strange thing but as you get older you start to recognise feelings and situations you've experienced before – existential déjà vu, if you like. The feelings I felt facing a major decision at 57 were the same as those I'd felt a long time ago – at the moment I'd been poised to strike out independently from my parents. That too was a decision coloured by an impending, inevitable death, although there was less for me to lose then in a material sense and everything to gain. Unlike now, I wasn't making the decision alone because in 1975 I was leaving home to get married. I got married on my 20th birthday.

I hope my generation of women is the last to grow up with an overriding principle that they must please, and please everyone, hard-wired into their brain. It's a burdensome thing to believe that your only role as a woman is to be the assistant stage manager in life's theatre – to support the star turn, the inevitable husband who has in turn been brought up to believe he has a divine right to run everything and that he is *never* wrong. But that is the way things were back then and it's crippling for a woman in today's world to have to carry that legacy. Aside from a general lack of opportunity, I wonder if that's why so many of us went on to become secretaries, nurses, teachers? We were taught to be good wives and mothers, to care and to serve. There are worse things I suppose but with a young girl's career advice usually running along the lines of 'Have you ever thought about being a hairdresser/telephonist/nanny?' surely at least a few prospective female neuroscientists or forklift drivers must have had their professional ambitions smothered at birth.

Certainly in the Midlands of the late 1960s, if you showed any academic determination or skill you ran the risk of being regarded as an unnatural swot and a freak of nature. I have in my mind a roll-call of at least half a dozen of my schoolmates who were denied university by their fathers on the basis that it would be a waste of time to educate a woman – fathers could do that then. I would ask any woman today who does not think herself a feminist to consider whether she could live as we did 40 years ago.

When the second wave of feminism gained traction in the '70s and the prospect of something different and better began to materialise, it brought with it an opportunity to break from the pattern. I wasn't a particularly earnest feminist at the time but I liked the idea that my life didn't have to be what everyone else said it should be, that I could meet it on my own terms. Here was a chance to decide for myself what my future would be and what I worked out for myself then surely laid the foundations for my personal ideologies now.

My early feminist tendencies caused a spot of bother at home because they were contradictory to everything my parents believed was right and proper for a genteel young woman. In my teens I certainly didn't think of myself 'genteel', with so much going on out in the big wide world there was nothing further from my mind – I wanted to try it all and I wasn't prepared to wait for permission. When I look back on my own small struggles to change what was inexplicably set in stone I can see why I am the way I am and why I choose, for the most part, to quietly work things out for myself, in my own way. I suppose I was a fairly typical adolescent really and this is what I remember again in middle age: that feeling of rebellion; that I didn't want to do something just because somebody else said I should, that it was expected or that it was my 'duty'. Even then I knew that what I was expected to do or be would leave me feeling suffocated.

Ironically, this time in my life when I should be enjoying greater freedoms is also a time when I feel considerable pressure to conform to the expectations of others, to be what society expects a middle-aged woman to be. Since when has it been the law that all middle-aged women must look and behave a certain way, or like the same things? Quite often now I find my hackles go up and I determinedly take the opposite tack just for the hell of it – I will *not* be told how I should be.

To push back against the model of the staid and stolid matron causes a good deal of pearl clutching, most often among the young, which is odd but perhaps a sign they prefer the comfort and reassurance of predictability after all. To give in to this pressure, to passively fall in with and support this daft stereotype is just lazy and ultimately it will not give you the life you want either.

There is some justification for the oft-repeated middle-aged mantra 'I know what I like' (which is after all an expression of wisdom gained) but if there's one thing we should have learned by now it's that you *never* know. And you may not always be able to have what you know you like. You have to be prepared for anything: prepared to compromise or make changes; to know how to choose which battles to fight and which to let pass. And you must also have a Plan B, solidly based in your experience of what worked before, balanced by what didn't, and powered by your own ambitions for your own future. To put yourself in the driving seat, to draw up such a plan, you will need to think back a long way, maybe right back to the beginning …

In our family there was me, and there were my two brothers – one older and one younger. Our mother and father had been on the threshold of adulthood when they were caught up in the Second World War. My mum had been an only daughter too but she was also an only child who was sheltered and protected by her parents. Her bit for the war effort was working in a Worcestershire munitions factory – the first time she'd ever been away from home. She fairly vibrated with distress whenever she talked about it, so she didn't. With the benefit of hindsight I imagine that her 'refinements' and naivety left her vulnerable to bullying. I also discovered, long after her death, that mum had been an accomplished amateur pianist. I was shocked when I found this out – in all the time I'd spent learning to play the recorder, the clarinet and the guitar mum never once mentioned she could read music, let alone play the piano. There was never a piano in the house. But then in so many ways my mother was a closed book.

While mum was packing bullets, my father was in the Pacific on an aircraft carrier. He was seventeen when he joined the navy and only really spoke about it, to me at least, in later life. Dad always had a powerful sense of responsibility. He was the eldest son of an architect, an architect who had spent much of his life battling his own demons with (I assume) a whisky bottle. Whatever his poison, he finished up an alcoholic – so dad, I suppose, felt responsible for his mother, younger brother and sister. I never knew my grandfather – he drank himself into an early grave before I was born. Perhaps life just didn't live up to his expectations. Apart from a few photographs and the knowledge that he played golf off an impressive handicap of six, that is all I know of grandpa.

Mum's parents were also unknowable to a large extent and here again I never knew my grandfather, who died suddenly before we were introduced. After the war dad met and married my mother, became a policeman and looked after his family and the community, although he once told me that what he really wanted to do was be a farmer. Dad wasn't a big one for talking either.

I arrived after a seven-year gap. Mum was delighted with her daughter, my older brother not so much. Mum curled my hair and dressed me in pretty dresses because that's what you did in the 1950s and '60s. But being a frilly, girlie girl didn't fit with the way I saw life, not when there were trees to be climbed and newts to be captured. Whenever I misbehaved, my older brother told me the doctor had brought me in a bag and I could easily be sent back. Nonetheless I was always up trees, playing cricket or pond dipping and there weren't many weeks when I wasn't in trouble for something or other. My first question whenever I got caught bang to rights was usually 'Why?' I wanted to know why what I'd done was wrong or dangerous or occasionally both but the response was usually something along the lines of 'Because I say so'.

The Moors Murders hit the headlines when I was nine and it was the first time I became aware that grown-ups will not always have your best interests at heart. That mugshot of Myra Hindley glaring out of the television screen or from the front page of a newspaper scared me witless. My father, as a policeman, was well placed to answer my questions but when I asked my parents why, they refused to discuss it, intending no doubt to protect me from the horror. The smoky conjurings my imagination produced were formless and, in their way, far worse.

Terrible and vivid nightmares followed – the first time I remember being afraid of what I couldn't comprehend.

This pattern of not talking about things was reinforced over and over again until it became set. I remember lending my Dr White's book on the facts of life – which my mother had discreetly covered in brown paper – to my school friend because it answered a fair few of the 'whats' and 'whys' we'd both been wondering about, but then I landed in terrible trouble when she showed it to her mum, who told my mum and I got a good hiding. No one told me why – only that I should be ashamed of myself. When I was older and wanted to go to Northern Soul dances in the next village or to see Marc Bolan at the De Montfort Hall I was told no but of course never why. As is the way with teenagers, I went anyway but dad had a spy network to rival SMERSH – the disadvantage of being the daughter of the local bobby – and he generally knew what I'd been up to before I even got home (generally 30 minutes late, which was about as far as I could push it). Interrogation after the event got them nowhere – by that time Torquemada would have struggled to get anything out of me because I had learned, and was still learning, by example.

I embarked on the usual juvenile experiments with alcohol, which resulted in some fairly tense 30-minutes-after-the-deadline homecomings. I'd always thought having a drink was something nice: my nan liked a nip of cherry brandy; my mum enjoyed the occasional sherry and got giggly at Christmas; dad liked a pint. Best of all was my favourite 'aunt' up the road who used to greet me with, 'Hello Hell! Fancy a gin? Oh, you can't. You're only NINE!' Probably pissed already, she roared with laughter and I thought she was hilarious. When I got round to trying it I found I liked the fuzziness and the way a drink knocked the sharp corners off my teenage angst. There were many dire parental warnings but no one mentioned my alcoholic grandfather (which would at least have shed some light on it) and no one told me what happened if you drank too much. According to my usual *modus operandi* I got shit-faced and sick as a parrot on cider and whisky one night, which answered that question quite nicely.

Independent exploration became the way I navigated through life. I gave up asking because no one would tell me. I looked at mum with her coffee mornings, twice-weekly shopping, flower arranging and rigid meal schedules (Sunday roast, Tuesday rissoles, fish on Friday) and decided that must not be me. Unless someone could satisfactorily explain to me why things had to be the grown-up way I was going to do things my way. As a result I got to know myself pretty well and indirectly I got to know a bit about feminism, which was a good match for my opinions about independence, the strength of women and (generally) idiot men.

Feminism in the Midlands of the 1970s seems a different sort of feminism to the kind we have now. Sexism was very much the order of the day and was so prevalent and in your face that it took a bit of adjustment to see it as something other than just the way life was. In an office environment for example, a female employee would generally find herself regarded as an amusing diversion by her male colleagues and any shortcomings (physical or otherwise) would be discussed openly in front of her and with anyone else who happened to be around. We were sex objects, baby machines and housekeepers – no one took us seriously in the workplace. In my first office job I couldn't do the filing without getting felt up by a revolting creature called Lance who used to lie in wait between 'M' and 'O' for unsuspecting secretaries. (Lance had a habit of drumming his long fingernails on desks and cabinets as he went on his merry way and to this day that sound makes me shudder.) A woman without a husband couldn't get a mortgage, a bank loan or anything else to set her up in an independent life. If a salesman called he would ask, 'Is your husband at home, love?' taking it for granted that you were far too fluffy to know your own mind regarding cavity wall insulation/insurance/buying a new duster. Working mothers were frowned upon and you usually worked until you became pregnant, giving it up at 28 weeks before you looked too pregnant and reminded all the men what sex was really about, which caused problems later when we wanted our jobs back. In fact it was considered perfectly normal at an interview to be asked about your marital status and plans for a family. Different territories for men and women were very clearly delineated, with business, breadwinning and decisions for the former; raising a family, running the home and endless domestic fussing for the latter. If it sounds feudal that's because it was, and I wasn't sure I wanted any of it – I wanted independence and escape.

I spent a good deal of time trying to escape. I was often at friends' houses where there was greater freedom and more social input. I once left mum a note begging her to send me to boarding school (I blame my *Malory Towers* addiction); the note came back with 'I don't think so' written on the bottom with a 'x'. Daft really, because whenever I went away on a school trip, I'd be crippled with homesickness before I lost sight of our house. Perhaps there was a more conventional girl in there after all.

When, in the early '70s, my mum was taken into hospital for what I was told would be a 'small' operation I was away at a festival. Whether dad was deliberately playing it down so as not to frighten me I shall never know but when I got back I was told the news that mum had colon cancer and it was most likely terminal. It was a terrible shock. I remember sitting at my desk and shaking. I'd had no idea.

People remember certain events as being the end of something, or the beginning. The knowledge of and coping with mum's illness for me were like a door closing on childhood. The next two-and-a-half years were grim and everything changed. My rebellions ceased and I acquired that essential female accomplishment of being 'biddable'; I went to secretarial college instead of university so that I would have something 'to fall back on'; I got married and I helped dad look after mum. Everything I thought I wanted I put away into a mental file marked 'pending'.

We all have this kind of stuff to deal with, and deal with it we do, but do we learn from it? Unless we think about it, the answer is probably not. Once it's over it becomes 'shit that happens' and we prefer not to look back on times that tested us so thoroughly and were so painful to live through. We put the memories away in a box and close the lid, firmly. I did learn something from the dislocation caused by my mother's death, although it would be more accurate to say it reinforced something I already knew: that I did not like not knowing why something had to be, and I never liked being dealt a curveball because it meant not being in control. I learned that without asking the right questions and receiving truthful answers, the right decision – an informed one – won't be made. Mistakes, on the other hand, often will. You might think I should have cottoned on to this already but I was young, a bit stupid, and I lacked the experience to work it out. Despite my best efforts I'd grown up a bit sheltered, like my mum. I was, along with so many of my generation, sent out into the world naive and clueless. But it was no one's fault really. It was simply the times we lived in.

What a wonderful thing is hindsight. No, really, it is. I can source a lot of my subsequent cock-ups to learning the 'lessons' that a) personal stuff is never discussed; b) if you want to know 'why' you have to interrogate people aggressively; and c) the way to a quiet life is not to exercise your own free will but to put up, shut up and do as you're told … whether you feel like it or not. But I also gained valuable lessons in keeping calm and carrying on, control-ling a volatile temperament, and learned that sometimes things happen for no logical reason. I learned that you should *always* have that Plan B. Benjamin Disraeli's quote 'prepare for the worst and hope for the best' fits the human condition perfectly.

The usual preparation for adulthood followed by my generation was an education, a couple of years in work (husband hunting), followed by marriage (to 'Tony from Accounts') and children (which meant giving up work, becoming wholly dependent on Tony and coincidentally giving up your National Insurance contributions – something else that tripped us up further down the line). There was in all likelihood not going to be another opportunity to remake yourself or better tailor your life until you reached the (hopefully) safe haven of middle age. The hiatus of our sixth decade is, we are told, when we can expect our thoughts to turn to what might have been – and what still might be, because now we have time and opportunity. There is far more opportunity in the 21st century than there ever was in the 20th ... we are told. What we are *not* told is that a good deal of what we could and should be doing is infected with and shut down by ageism. In fact it's worse than that because this ageism has sexism running through the middle like a stick of Blackpool rock.

Before she died, and in her own way, given it was the 1970s, my mother had a tentative crack at a touch of 'seizing the day' herself. She took a part-time job in a jeweller's, earning her own money for the first time in 30 years (although she would never have thought of it in those terms) and she learned to drive. She even passed her driving test. OK, she passed on the ninth attempt but to keep trying like that took guts and I confess I hadn't thought she had it in her.

From what I remember of my mother's approach to achieving middle age in the early 1970s she also did a lot of what I'm doing now – looking retrospectively at life. I remember her worries about her weight – she had always been petite but the goal then was to remain a size 12. (Goodness only knows what she would have made of size 000.) I remember the agonies of embarrassment she went through over the menopause, although naturally we never talked about it and it took a good deal of putting two and two together before I was able to work out that mum's problem was The Change. (That I was adolescent as she was menopausal was appalling timing but explains a lot. I hadn't realised this either until last year.)

Learning to drive and taking a part-time job was the 1970s equivalent of what so many of us do at this life axis – mum was starting to think about what she was going to do with the next part of her life when there was just her and dad. That she didn't make it through but was clobbered by rogue genes in her 50s not only proves my point about being prepared for anything but also drives home the important message that you should always – *always* – make the most of what you have.

A friend-of-a-friend decided to save money and repair the roof himself after the Great Storm of 1987 swept through and dislodged some slates. Mindful of the dangers, he tied a length of rope securely around his waist and threw the other end over the apex of the roof and into the front garden, where his son was waiting to tie it off securely. That done he went up the ladder and started work. After about an hour his wife shouted up that she was popping out to the shops. As his wife inched the car out into the road he began to inch upwards. As his wife accelerated he shot up the roof at speed. He said he experienced a brief moment of clarity about exactly where his son had tied the other end of the rope at about the same time as he made a determined but futile bid to seize hold of the chimney. Fortunately he landed in a flowerbed. *Un*fortunately he broke both legs and his left arm, knocked out a few teeth and spent the best part of a month in hospital. To add insult to injury, he dislodged a couple of dozen more slates and part of the chimney on his way down.

I know I shouldn't laugh.

As a parable about the perils of assuming things, this story fits surprisingly well. Did you, while you were going about your business, ever spare a thought for how unforeseen circumstances could send you crashing down to earth? Having made a few assumptions of my own, I didn't think about it either, or at least not until I began to gain momentum during my own downward slide; and yes it did hurt when I landed – it hurt a lot. I should have known this. After all there have been a few downward slides over the years, some further than others.

I've gone through life in the permanent hope that something will turn up. This is what we call optimism. However, optimism does have a downside in that it doesn't allow preparation for the setbacks that will surely come about in any lifetime. In my case, and despite indications to the contrary, I didn't anticipate a divorce after fifteen years of marriage and three children. The rocketing rise in the divorce rate is an important factor in the way my generation will live in later years and I think it's caught us on the hop. Certainly I, like my mother, believed that when you got married that was it. That it turned out not to be was unexpected. How many of us are similarly facing life as middle-aged single women – and happily so – but find that whatever our own plans may be the world out there isn't prepared for us?

After the divorce I moved swiftly from an affluent lifestyle to having nothing, not even my children. (This was an epic downward slide to rock bottom, more or less.) When after a lengthy legal tussle I was finally awarded custody I had barely two pennies to rub together. Somehow or other we managed but, with no maintenance to speak of, finding a way of earning a living and supporting the four of us was imperative. At the time I was working as a medical secretary in Leicester but the cottage I rented was in the countryside (where it was cheaper). Because my girls had had such an awful time I felt I needed to be around for them. I needed to be around from a practical point of view too. A forward-thinking NHS manager gave me a massive leg-up when he suggested that if I had a computer at home then we could work something out. So I picked up dictation tapes and took them home to type up. I did this all around the hospital in most of the different clinical specialties: wherever there was a backlog, or a secretary off sick or on holiday, I took on the workload. I was, in effect, a freelance medical secretary. This represents a perfect example of 'something turning up' and I will be forever grateful to that man because without his willingness to be flexible I don't know what we would have done.

I wish today's recruiters could understand that there is more than one way to skin the employment cat. The workplace and employment market have changed to such a degree since I got that break that if anything finding work should be easier than ever, and particularly for older women who so frequently find themselves caught between care responsibilities at both ends of the generational scale. Of all the buzzwords flying about modern human resources departments today, 'flexibility' seems to be the one most used but least employed. Unimaginative employers have their age blinkers firmly on and skills and experience go to waste. It creates dreadful hardship.

Over the eight years I worked at home, in addition to my freelance work at the hospital, I used all my skills, creative and practical, to keep us afloat: I took on commissions for wedding dresses, I took on art work, I worked part-time in a deli and I wrote copy. We were never well off but we had a home and food to eat, I could pay the bills and we were together – and that was all that mattered.

Boom and bust seems to be a pattern with me, as I believe it is for many people. When things are going well you forget the hard times but there is an awful inevitability to the way they come back round again and we would do well to remember that. Although that's easier said than done.

Once the children were old enough I went back to working full-time in the NHS. And then I lost my job and that's where this chapter started – when I began looking for work in London. The bit prior to starting my new life in the capital was financially tough. But I'd fallen foul of a bullying manager at the hospital and so the first step towards my new future was when I decided to hit back and take the health authority to a tribunal. After I fought and won my case for unfair dismissal I had a little money to get me started again and that was all the leg-up I needed.

Living and working in London, once I found my feet, was another spell of 'boom' and it happened at an age when many women are beginning to slow down. When I started again in my mid-40s I just felt I had more to offer, and besides, I wanted more. I had things to prove to myself. It was important to me to defeat the psychological damage of being victimised and sacked. I cared a lot about the humiliation I'd gone through. It was important to me to prove I wasn't useless. I wanted to be able to say, 'Hah! So I'm pretty good at this PA-ing lark after all.' And stick two fingers up to the woman who used to call me 'the skinny bitch'. After I'd done that, that's when I'd think about what I might do later to support myself when I was older. But then there was the next thing, and the next thing, and I never quite got round to it. By the time I arrived at my 57-year-old wobble it was really a bit late – with foresight I could have already had wheels on my 'Third Age' career and been revving under starter's orders.

I'd always thought that once I stopped taking on the world I would fall back on my creative skills. After all, in the past they provided me with a pretty decent living and as a bonus they made me happy. Me, the writer, had been a personal ambition ever since I created my first cartoon strip for the school magazine but I never really did anything about it other than fiddle around with an opinion piece here and some theatre programme copy there. I was nervous about being judged on my style and ideas, about pushing myself out into the spotlight, which was unknown territory, and where perhaps I would lose control of my life. To be a writer would involve a certain amount of self-promotion, which I also found awkward – I could hear my mother whispering, 'Don't show off, darling'. I was afraid of trying and failing. I was sure I *would* fail and to fail meant extinguishing my hopes for a better future.

When I was asked to write a weekly online fashion column for older women at the *Guardian* I did it because I believed I should; after all I'd been banging on for long enough about the way we were neglected. It's interesting that I should take that view because earlier in this chapter I made a clear point about our generation being brought up to please, to be unselfish. That upbringing meant that I always found it easier to do something for me personally under the protective camouflage of doing it for someone else, so in this case I told myself I was doing it for women like me and not for *me* me. It was a self-deception that worked. After all, I could move heaven and earth for my family or my boss but for myself? Not so much.

For a number of reasons I decided I wanted to be anonymous: I wanted to minimise conflict with my 'day' job but also it might not be any good and if no one knew 'The Invisible Woman' was Helen Walmsley-Johnson, I was giving myself the freedom to fail. I wanted to gauge the response from one step removed and it seemed to me the only way to guarantee an honest opinion. I didn't even tell my boss, or at least not for three months or so.

When an agent signed me up and we talked about writing this book, all the vague ideas I'd had about the shape my later life could take began to look as though they might be achievable after all.

But I loved my job so much that I didn't want to leave – or, perhaps more accurately, it was the regular salary I didn't want to leave, but I wouldn't admit that to myself. It would mean striking out into the unknown and starting yet *again* from the ground up. It would mean tearing up my original plan to stay put at the *Guardian* until I retired, which felt a bit like backing down and I'd given up backing down because it felt too much like failure. I had another thought: what if, when I retired in 2020, I'd left it too late to become a writer and the moment had passed forever? What if I wasted all the opportunities landing in my lap to do this now, when I could (just about) still start again?

As is my way, I stopped thinking and powered on trying to push through doubt, avoid making a decision and doing everything I was asked to do until one day I simply couldn't do it any more. I hit a wall, exhausted. It was entirely my own fault. I broke myself. In the end my health decided it for me and I had to take a forced break to rest and recover. For three months I seemed to do nothing but sleep and then I slowly began to acknowledge that things couldn't continue as they were. I had the best set of circumstances I could ever hope for to push out on my own and see if I really could make it as a writer. Terrified or not, the obvious thing to do was stop faffing, apply for voluntary redundancy, carpe the fuck out of the diem and get on with it.

That still makes the decision sound easier than it was. It sounds daft but I really had sleepwalked through my 50s, waking up when I was 57 and thereby frightening myself half to death. What would happen to me now, as a middle-aged single woman? How would I be able to support myself with a decent standard of living? The small pension pot I'd scraped together would help but not much. I wanted to spend time with my father but we were both stroppy and didn't always get on. I struggled to deal with the fact that he was dying. Within six months two friends, one older than me, one younger, had been handed a similarly devastating prognosis. As far as your own mortality goes, cancer striking three times in your immediate circle certainly makes you think about what you'd regret *not* doing while you still had the chance. I was already older than my mum had been when she died. I began to not exactly *not* be afraid but to see the next 20 years as a benediction. In terms of my mum and my friends, young and old, I was already on borrowed time and I couldn't allow myself to waste any more of it. That was the final nudge. I calculated the redundancy money would keep me going for eighteen months if I was careful. I would get a part-time job to keep me afloat and make it last longer. I had a weekly column, an agent, a decent address book and enough money to get me started. I owed it to myself to at least give it a shot.

A year later – two weeks after my father's death – I discovered that for once there was something London hadn't been leading the rest of the country on. While I'd taken into account the global recession and the inevitable gap in earnings while I got myself up and running I hadn't planned on the workplace ageism I'd encountered in the Midlands fifteen years before catching up with me again in the capital. I had promptly registered with four recruitment agencies – two of whom knew me well from my PA role at the *Guardian*. They all raved about my CV and what excellent experience I had and they all promised to be in touch. I attended a couple of interviews for part-time maternity cover. And then there was silence – a whole eighteen months of it. Occasionally there were polite telephone conversations and email exchanges but no further interviews.

While the agencies were supposedly working on my behalf I was also searching, looking for something to help me ease into this new life. I did it enthusiastically until I got within striking distance of an unbelievable 500 applications and I began to lose hope. Then to cap it all, one well-respected agency and the one which knew me best told me that the recruiters for one of the jobs I'd asked about were looking for someone 'more up and coming … presumably as opposed to "been and gone"', I laughed (before I hung up and threw my phone across the room). This, it turns out, is the new face of ageism. I grew very weary of these opaque statements from professionals who know perfectly well that they mustn't say anything overt about my (by now) 58 years while at the same time intimating that I had more chance of rowing the Atlantic single-handed than successfully finding another job.

A kind of horrible downward impetus starts to build for someone when they tumble into this web of problems. I, in common with many others I spoke to, went from feeling confident and reasonably assured about my future to feeling worry and anxiety blossom in my insides (inevitably around three in the morning). As my savings dwindled I considered signing on for benefits and found, also in common with many others I spoke to, that a mixture of pride and shame wouldn't allow me to. I could sell some of my things and, somehow, I would manage. I began to contemplate which child or friend or relative I might be forced to ask for help, even as far as giving me a roof over my unemployed, useless middle-aged head, but most of my contemporaries were in a similar bind themselves. I began to see my credit rating collapse as I started to default on bills and I dreaded the arrival of the post, the ring of the phone or a buzz on the doorbell. I began to feel very afraid, about everything. I couldn't afford to buy new make-up, or get a haircut or pay any bus/train fares. If I'd been lucky enough to snag a job interview I would have had to walk the seven miles into town (I needn't have worried, there weren't any).

I began to go out of my way to avoid seeing myself in a mirror because I looked dishevelled and nervy and full of self-doubt, and it damaged my confidence further. My careful records of which jobs I'd applied for began to seem pointless and tailed off after my 500th application but there was still a flicker of hope – until that too finally puttered out and I began to wonder what would come next, how much further I would fall and how much longer I could hold on. It was when I could no longer afford food or rent that I found myself doing uncharacteristic things ...

As far as I was able, I had started campaigning for women like me and it was because of this activity that just before Christmas I found myself at a coffee morning in the House of Commons wondering whether anyone would notice if I pocketed a couple of mince pies. That day I'd spent all my money on the train fare to get there. There was only 20p in my purse for emergencies and I was starving. At the same coffee morning I met a woman who'd not eaten for three days to afford the train fare, which only goes to show that there's always someone worse off than yourself. So there we both were, busting a (rumbling) gut to attend an important event for women and gender equality, standing shoulder to shoulder with half the shadow cabinet and both of us contemplating some light-fingered canapé thievery because we couldn't afford to eat. It would be funny if it weren't so tragic.

I can't stop worrying about how it is for other women like me so I'm trying to somehow do something about it. It takes time and effort but it also means having to set aside all my silly ingrained hang-ups about shyness, self-effacement, not making a fuss and being laughed at. I have to get myself out there. I've experienced enough to know perfectly well what I'm talking about but the more I've gone out and about and met other women and talked on the radio and written about it, the more I've discovered that I am so very much not alone.

I have to ask, what happened to my generation that we've forgotten about the struggles of 50 years ago when we were all in it together and we campaigned and fought for women's rights? The world now is every bit as outrageously biased and unfair as the one we faced then. To assume that because you're all right now you always will be is a terrible, disastrous mistake. For any woman in her 50s there is very little standing between her and disaster and that will be the case as long as we allow gender-based ageism to exist.

If this all sounds a little negative then take comfort from the fact that I have also met many women who have changed course completely at this point in their lives and done it successfully. Thank goodness for the women who have quietly and determinedly got on with making the life they want for themselves despite the patronising, 'funny age' jokes and 'midlife crisis' dismissals. Why does anything unexpected in our lives have to be attributed to our hormones, as though we had no free will of our own? Doesn't it make you spitting mad? It's just the same sort of nonsense we used to get when we were young women in the 1970s, when if we forgot ourselves and expressed an opinion it was blamed on 'the time of the month'. This is *exactly* the same thing. We made things better once and we need to do it again. Otherwise our daughters and granddaughters will still be facing these difficulties, this discrimination, when they reach our age.

3
WTF

'You may have a fresh start any moment you choose, for this thing that we call "failure" is not the falling down, but the staying down.'
—MARY PICKFORD

If 2013 was a bad year, 2014 was shaping up to be a lot worse. I'd already lost one friend and my father to cancer but by April last year I'd lost yet another friend to the same wretched disease, followed by my dear old cat, Titus. It sounds stupid but losing the cat felt like the last straw – I couldn't even afford to pay the vet to put him to sleep and had to arrange for his death by instalments. I got home with an empty cat basket, drank what was left of the whisky and howled, literally, with grief. Titus's brother, Pushkin, was completely thrown to find himself suddenly alone and solo cat-in-residence. He and Titus had never been apart and he missed his protective big brother a lot, roaming the flat day and night calling for him.

At around the same time my stepmother, who'd never quite recovered from the sorrow of losing my father, received her own diagnosis – cancer again. With exquisite timing my landlord decided he wanted me to move out and I can see why – I'd been in that flat for almost fifteen years and I was paying less rent than he would be able to get for it in a buoyant London market if he hoicked me out and brought in a new tenant. So he began hoicking.

Pressure piled on pressure. This was a bad time, one of the worst. Times like these are inclined to send me, or anyone, a bit bonkers. I found myself living two half-lives. In one I would be in front of a camera being filmed for a documentary, speaking to a room full of people, attending conferences, interviewing, talking to politicians about the plight of older women or researching what I hoped would be a book. In the other life I was sitting in my flat or roaming Greenwich Park, thinking desperate thoughts and wondering how the hell I was going to get through this. When I filed an article to the *Guardian* that began by using Tolkien's Ents as a metaphor for older women, although it seemed entirely logical to me at the time, with hindsight it clearly wasn't, and I began to worry that I was losing my grip entirely. The editor who'd commissioned the piece was too kind to say what she really thought and, although she knew nothing of the state I was in, patiently took me through re-shaping it. One day I'll thank her properly for that.

It's hard to tell people when this kind of thing is happening to you, to talk about how you're feeling, but of course you should. I didn't though, because I'd never acquired the habit. Instead I offered the excuse of not sleeping, which was sort of true but it wasn't the whole story, just a convenient barricade to hide behind. Occasionally I tweeted a little of my misery and a welcome gust of support blew in through the tiny Twitter window I'd opened into my life. I suppose I felt ashamed by how quickly and how far I'd fallen but the truth is that this is what happens to so many of us in our 50s. Not only are we coping with ourselves and all the changing emotions and fluctuating feelings middle age can bring but we're dealing with the symptoms (sometimes severe) of peri-, post- or actual menopause. We're caring for grandchildren or parents and holding down a job at the same time, or trying to find work in a hostile market, and we're battling through it all pale and tight-lipped and not telling a soul about any of it.

I began to blame myself for waiting so long to think about moving out of London, or rather for thinking it and not doing anything. There was a reason I was still there though: I was laying down the foundations for whatever I was going to do next to earn a living and since a job was not forthcoming then writing it would have to be. Writing was my original plan and it did at least earn me something. Writing was what I wanted to do but I couldn't afford to do it in the city. But by then I couldn't afford to move either.

This is exactly the kind of situation when a life manual or therapist will tell you to make a list of the pros and cons of your intended course of action. This is the accepted wisdom and, yes, quite a sensible thing to do in that it makes you focus and think, work it out sensibly and come up with some kind of a plan. I prefer to adopt my own, more rousing terminology so I call the cons WTF (what the fuck?); the pros we can call ... whatever the opposite of 'what the fuck' is. Let's say it's Joy. In an old notebook

I recently turned up a WTF list of age-related things I wrote down a couple of years ago:

- Knees, knuckles, elbows and other baggy bits that should be pointy
- Vaginal lifts/rejuvenating vulvo-vaginal fillers. Fuck.
- 'Anti ageing' – see also 'renew', 'perfect', 'combat', 'fight', 'forever young' …
- Big pants – also bras
- Shopping for clothes in an actual shop, not the Internet – feel like a freak
- Indigestion
- Sleep – lack of
- Sweatiness
- Whiskers
- Sex – lack of
- Death
- Money – lack of
- I'm 57 … WTF?

The Joy list is shorter:

- I have learned to do things on my own – and I like it
- I know what I like
- I can work most stuff out because most of it I've done before
- I really like my face *as it is*
- I no longer give a fuck what anyone else thinks about me (liberating)
- Nobody *is* thinking about me (also liberating)

... and it's mostly full of 'I', which now I think is interesting. Perhaps this shows that at the time my focus was shifting from looking out for everyone else to looking after me – not that I was aware of it; it just seemed to happen. I think more 'me' focus at this stage of life is a very good thing for any woman. A 'sod you' attitude can carry you a long way.

I have a bit of a thing for lists; I make a list of everything I need to pack before I go on holiday and then I never look at it again. I did the same thing with revision for school exams – a) write it all down; b) never look at it again. This is how I remember things. (The only exception to this, obviously, is a shopping list when without fail I come home without the one thing I went shopping for in the first place.)

Either way, to say that a lot changed in the two years following that particular WTF list would be something of an understatement. My itchy feet got a lot worse for one thing, and for two successive New Year's Eves I raised a glass to absent friends and promised myself this would positively, *absolutely* be the last NYE spent in my London flat with Jools Holland on the telly and the cat asleep beside me on the sofa. I didn't mind 'alone' but I did mind the feeling that I should have moved on by now. For two wretched years I'd been stymied, unable to work out how to find my way through a forest of difficulties, real and imagined, and I couldn't shake off the fear that whatever I did, whichever way I jumped, it would be wrong.

Next I began blaming myself for everything, thinking it was all my own stupid fault. I felt so ashamed that I had apparently made a terrible error of judgement in taking redundancy when I did. This, of course, is nonsense. I know that now. I had made my decision based on the information I had available to me and it was a sensible one … at the time. I could not have known – because no one was taking much notice of it then – that in doing that I was accidentally retiring myself. Or that 'catastrophic early retirement' (as it is now called) is the trap a good proportion of the 3.3 million 50- to 64-year-olds who are 'economically inactive'* have fallen into – just like me, but that didn't stop me beating myself up over it. Eventually though, my self-pity drained away and I got angry. In life I've often found that being properly angry will power me through something horrible with the smooth efficiency of a turbo-charged engine so 'angry' was a good thing for me to be just then.

To pay my rent I pawned the camera I'd saved up for. It has, of course, gone forever because I could never scrape enough together to get it back again – that hurt. I learned to dislike and mistrust the deceptively amiable atmosphere in the spaces between locked cabinets and glass-fronted kiosks where I queued with everyone else, all of us clutching whatever possessions we considered we could temporarily (or permanently) do without. There were a lot of us, and the need is clear, but this isn't the work of some public-spirited philanthropist – it's a way for the unscrupulous to fleece what little there is off those who can least afford it. The easy nonchalance of the man

---

* Office of National Statistics, 2014

behind the desk is too professional, too slick and too brittle, and I don't think he likes being there any more than I do. Our reward for parking our dignity is the comfort of a wodge of cash in hand, even if it's only there for the time it takes to walk to the bank and pay a few bills. Don't underestimate this fleeting self-respect, but the relief doesn't last – days if you're lucky, hours if you're not. You're paying for the privilege with the interest charged on your television/food mixer/granny's watch and as the interest creeps higher and the chance of redeeming your ticket recedes into the distance, your friendly pawn shop gets a bargain to sell on. It's a win-win situation ... for them.

I braved the council offices and applied for housing benefit. That's 'benefit' in the loosest sense because no one must know you have it – and if your landlord finds out, your arse will be bounced out on to the pavement so fast you might as well have announced you have anthrax. The council office staff, to me at any rate, were kind and helpful and sorted me out quickly but there were plenty who were less fortunate and plenty of hefty security staff who weren't exactly standing around idle. I came out close to tears (gratitude) and with the tiniest sliver of hope because whatever my feelings were about my tiny flat, the noise and hopeless neighbours, it had been my home for almost fifteen years, and that counts for something.

I'd moved to this flat at another 'life's painted me into a corner' time. When I moved down from Leicester with everything I possessed in a few bin bags I'd started in a tiny Stratford house share with five other people; that's quite a challenge for someone in their 40s and used to living on their own but I stuck it for six months until it seriously started to drive me mad. Finding this quiet, sunny flat was an enormous stroke of luck and it was where I started again for the umpteenth time. This little corner of South-East London was where I came to recover after a radical hysterectomy for early-stage cervical cancer. It's where I went to ground after my boyfriend dumped me. The tiny bathroom was where I'd sat in scalding water to get rid of the smell of a man I'd thought was a gentleman but who, for all his designer suits and lovely manners, turned out to be quite the opposite. These four walls were where I'd survived, dreamed and planned, and I'd sheltered inside them for the longest time I'd ever lived anywhere in my entire life. It's hard to leave somewhere like that even when you know you've outgrown it in more ways than mere cat-swinging space. It had been home and it contained memories. The thought of leaving it and starting again somewhere else gave me palpitations but it was time to move on. The question was how and to work that out I needed to buy myself just a little more time.

If any of this sounds depressingly familiar then be reassured that you are not alone. The kind of seismic change and crushing self-doubt I was experiencing seems to be something that happens to an awful lot of us at some point during our middle age – and I think it's meant to. If, like me, you drift through life with no proper plan (because who on earth makes a life plan in their 20s and sticks to it?) there will come a moment when you think, 'hang on ...' This moment will arrive at whatever point you decide to weigh up your life so far and to ask yourself whether you've got what you want from it. More often than not, you will do this when you reach some sort of natural hiatus, perhaps the one that occurs after children have grown up and gone, or you begin to acknowledge that despite the UK government's ever-receding threshold for state pensions, whatever now passes for a retirement date is a lot closer than you thought. This ruminative period is when you start mulling over how you'd *really* like to spend the next few years as opposed to merely marking time with the same old same old. You begin to think in terms of 'there must be more' and 'this might be my last chance to …'

With any luck that practical streak you've spent your life learning to listen to will take you to one side and gently point out that while you might well have the free will and time to do as you wish, you will likely still need to work to keep a roof over your head. It might then occur to you to try something that will ease you into it, to dip a toe into the alternative existential water, as it were, to see if it freezes your blood or is pleasantly warm. If, for example, there's something you've always wanted to try your hand at, now might be the time to give it a go – a career transition for this transitional phase of life, a step sideways into something that feels a better fit for when you yourself are not quite so lively. This is not turning your face to the wall or The Beginning of the End – it's sensible, practical and about thinking ahead to your midlife Plan B. You should, however, expect some negative 'incoming' because people do love to see the downside and anything to do with adjusting to your time of life tends to be seen as 'giving up'. Remember too that whatever anyone else tells you this is *not* your midlife crisis (more on that in the next chapter).

In the meantime, let's just consider the word 'alone' for a moment. Assuming you got married (like your parents), you probably also expected to stay married (like your parents). However, it's increasingly unlikely that this has proven to be the case. According to the Office for National Statistics, 22 per cent of marriages made in 1972 had ended in divorce by their fifteenth anniversary; for marriages made in 1997 the figure is higher at 33 per cent. That divorce figures overall are currently falling is perhaps more of an indication that marriage itself is less popular than that we are entering a period of rediscovered connubial bliss. We are now far more likely to simply cohabit (in which case the average duration of the relationship is something in the region of three-and-a-half years), and this is fine but can leave us high and dry legally and financially if we decide to go our separate ways. Meanwhile, those of us who are still married in their 50s have no cause for complacency, with divorce rates for men over 50 among the highest. Our generation is moving beyond the traditional role models of the past to a point where if we meet a couple celebrating over ten or fifteen years of marriage they deserve congratulating. Long marriages have become something of a rarity with 53 per cent ending in divorce before their 30th anniversary if the couple married at around age 20 – which we forget was quite common in the 1970s. Perhaps I should take comfort from being entirely average in this regard. But that's just divorce – the Grim Reaper also takes his share, lest we forget. My point is that none of us can assume entitlement to a life where coupledom continues smoothly forever after with nary a ripple, which is tough – indeed, heart-breaking – if you happen to be happy with the one you've got.

If you think about it realistically, all sorts of things can get in the way of your ongoing domestic nirvana and such things often draw a marriage or partnership to a natural conclusion during these middle years. So here's something else to think about: single occupancy in the UK has increased from 12 per cent of all households in 1961 to nearly 30 per cent in 2011, then upwards to 34 per cent in 2012. It seems to me that this upward trend will only continue. When the data collected by the Office for National Statistics (where would we be without them?) is analysed further, it shows that the biggest increase happens in the age group 45–64 with a slower rise in age group 65–74. The UK is third after Sweden and Germany in terms of solo living. Age groups 16–24, 25–44 and 75 and over remain more or less steady.

This shift suggests to me that something happens in middle age which creates a dramatic change in circumstances for quite a number of us and I would suggest it's got quite a lot to do with people wanting life on their own terms after decades of putting others first. It's probably always been like that, but the difference between this generation and the last is that now we have more opportunity to do something about it, with divorce far less stigmatising and much easier to obtain than it used to be. Whereas in the past it's generally fallen to the husband to initiate the end of a marriage it's now more likely to be the woman. In 2011 women initiated 66 per cent of the UK's divorces with over half of those divorces being granted on the grounds of their husband's 'unreasonable behaviour'. We're far less afraid of living on our own; in fact some of us actively seek it. This is relatively new for us when not all that long ago it was still jokily supposed (ho ho) that a typical lady living alone must be a sad spinster in desperate need of a husband but making do with a cat. (There was one who lived near us and my mother used to call her The Awful Warning.) It's also not all that long ago that women had relatively few legal rights – for example, the Court of Appeal only repealed the law permitting a pub or bar to refuse to serve unaccompanied women in 1982 so if you were single in the 1970s you couldn't even go to the pub for a solitary consoling drink. Thank goodness those days are gone. But somehow, for reasons I personally can't fathom having done it myself for well over a decade, living alone is still regarded as an odd thing for a woman to want to do of her own free will. It still seems to go against the grain: we're supposed to be selfless nurturers and not nurturers of ourselves.

As ever, advertisers, media and politicians are some way behind the curve on this, and in none of the many reports I've read on the plight of the 50- to 65-year-old woman in today's society is the fact that many women in this age group are supporting themselves on a single income taken into account. It is apparently more convenient for number-crunching to assume that all the middle-aged women surveyed are part of a mutually dependent, double income household. This worries me because those of us who are living this life are essentially lost statistics, which in turn means that nothing, or very little, is known about or done for us. As a result, and because our job prospects are now so poor, it's almost inevitable that we should struggle to support ourselves, whether we live alone through our own choice, as a result of the decisions of others or because of a particular set of circumstances.

On a more positive note, we have in recent years seen a rise in the number of women's housing cooperatives. That's interesting, because it shows that we lost statistics were the first to identify the problem and take practical steps to improve things in a way that is much more to our liking. And let's face it, such is the invisibility of the middle-aged woman that if we were to wait for anyone else to step up to the plate we'd be waiting a bloody long time.

Anyway ... for far too long I had kept hoping that someone somewhere would offer me one of the 500-odd jobs I'd applied for and then I'd get things straight again. It's that hope that kills you because it's what keeps you anchored to the spot long after you should have moved on.

Some of us have the capacity to embrace change and leap recklessly in while others dither about on the brink and worry. Ironically, in our middle years, when experience and life have provided us with bucket loads of backbone and native cunning, we suddenly begin questioning every-thing we thought we knew and believed in. Certainly I had a lot of one-sided nocturnal conversations with my cat last year as I attempted to theorise my way out of this mother of all messes. It really is the most wretchedly awful timing: our impulse is to change and adapt – it is, after all, nature's own survival strategy – but we're resistant and clutching tightly to that comfort blanket of familiarity I mentioned. We've done it so many times already ... Is it really fair to expect us to go through all that again, and at our time of life?

With my previous life change, when I packed up and moved to London in my mid-40s that was me feeling the fear and doing it anyway. I was sticking two fingers up at an inadequate provincial job market and at my own circle of disbelievers – the ones who said I'd lost the plot and the ones who asked if I'd really do it. Any grit and determination I showed at the time was the product of my stubborn refusal to back down and a boiling pit of anger, that useful rocket fuel. I'd show them. Of course I'd do it! And once I'd said that, it meant I had to do it. Once I'd done it and my new life began to flourish I had to contend with the envy-tinged 'oh, you're SO lucky' remarks. Luck had very little to do with it, I'd explain through gritted teeth, I *made* something happen ... me, *I* did. I decided what I had to do and it wasn't easy but I did it. I think I proved pretty conclusively that this girl was made of the strongest of the strong stuff, whatever anyone else might think. But mostly I did it for me. Was I terrified? You bet – and very helpful it was too.

Of course there's a world of difference between starting again with a family in tow, maybe post-divorce, and starting again on your own. Having done both I'd say that doing it with children was much easier because you're doing it more for them than you are for yourself – they provide you with the spur. I remember that everything I did then was with them in mind, to give them the best fresh start I possibly could and, with the usual burden of adult guilt in such situations, to make up for their parents being such a pair of deadbeats. Mine was an uncommonly messy divorce, which made creating a secure new family home much more of an imperative than it might have been otherwise. And once more, anger and a refusal to be beaten built me a decent engine with which to drive the rest.

This is again that generational thing, that legacy from the 1950s that said women had to make everything lovely for everyone else. It was only when I reached middle age that I cottoned on to it properly. When I was growing up at home (and between teenage rebellions) I tried to please my parents and my teachers; when I left home to get married I tried to please my parents, my husband and his parents; when I had children the list expanded to include my children's teachers, other parents and, of course, my daughters; when I went back to work it was all about impressing and pleasing my boss and my colleagues. My motivation was all about other people, so where was I in all this? Well, I suppose I was somewhere down near the bottom of the list and I got very good at putting myself there, using everyone else's needs as an excuse to avoid parking myself up front and centre.

One day, lying in the bath (I have some of my best thoughts lying in the bath) I had a moment of blinding clarity when I recognised that all my life I would far rather make a noble sacrifice than make a stand for something I wanted for *me*. It was easier that way. Giving something up bestows a feeling of having done something good, of having been the selfless one, but it's also a way of punishing yourself for wanting whatever it was in the first place – it's a form of masochism.

My generation were taught to squash the part of us that jumps up and down yelling 'But what about ME???' In time it becomes a reflex. Remember the recurring 'cream cake scene' in *Last of the Summer Wine* when the ladies are having one of their coffee morning war councils? A plate of very ordinary cakes would be passed around, with one oozing and delicious, generously proportioned cream bun in the middle. Everyone made a great show of selfless good manners, eyeing the bun with longing and grudgingly leaving it for someone else, and every time, without fail, that someone else was Nora Batty, who swiped the bun with an expression of deep satisfaction while the others gaped in shock.

What I'm saying is: FFS swipe the cream bun.

It's probably no surprise that I moved myself to London when I did. It happened at a time when my belief in the set of values I grew up with had been seriously called into question, when I was picked on and eventually forced out of my job with the NHS in Leicestershire.

Surely I must have known all along that there is a law of the jungle to the way we live, that people don't always behave decently and that they will lie and wriggle and cheat and do whatever they can to save their own skin.

I didn't *exactly* do the same thing but this time I did at least take the opportunity to stand up for myself when I couldn't accept what had been done to me. I fought back against the bully who'd made my life a misery, fought back angrily and hard and I won. In the process I learned that there is something profoundly empowering about making a stand for what you know is right and believe in, for taking not just what you need but what you want. Now I think about it, I can see that the whole nasty business gave me the courage to do something else I'd never done before: two months before I moved to London I went on holiday for the first time in twelve years – and I went by myself.

The air buffeting my face through the open window was hairdryer-hot. The horizon shimmered, hazy, copper red. Beneath my feet I could see the road to the mountains, the sounding-grander-than-it-was R203, whizzing past through rust holes in the floor of the elderly Mercedes. We sped on past scooters with boxes of chickens tied to the handlebars and three, sometimes four, passengers; past roadside bars with plastic buckets of cacti fermenting in the shade; past scrubby trees, sheep, goats, horses and an occasional camel. We whipped past in a swirling choke of dust, up and up, looping around and around dozens of hairpin bends that flung us out over vertiginous drops. We stopped to help a broken-down car, or rather the driver did – I sweated nervously on the turquoise fake fur seat – but, as he said, 'who else would stop here?'

After another hour or so we pulled in through a pair of tall iron gates and it was only after I'd checked in and been led through silent gardens to a tiny creeper-clad house, when I put down my bag and sat alone on a hard wooden bed, that *what the hell have you done?* trailed across behind my closed eyelids like a banner behind a light aircraft. Yes, what *had* I done – Morocco, in July and out of season, high in the Atlas Mountains and miles from anywhere. Temperatures in Marrakech hovered above the 40° mark and it wasn't much cooler here, at altitude. 'Look, Walmers,' I said to myself, 'if this really does turn out to be the stupidest thing you've ever done and you honestly can't hack it, you can always check out tomorrow and go somewhere else.' I couldn't. I didn't have enough money to do that, but it did feel a bit like that necessary Plan B. I'd give it 24 hours and see how it went.

That week, despite the shaky start, turned out to be one of the most profound experiences of my life. Chosen almost on the flip of a coin, it took me a long way out of my middle-aged comfort zone. It taught me that I could travel alone, and a little way off the beaten track, and that there was no harm in taking risks, as long as they were the calculated sort. And if it didn't work out, did it really matter all that much? I would still have learned something.

As it happened, once I'd caught the Moroccan vibe (it took less than twelve hours), learned to deal with the mutant insect life and the odd unfamiliar night noises, I really took to the place. There's a lot to be said for dining out under North African stars every night, for the weird orange landscape split apart by vivid green valleys that frothed and foamed with olive and almond trees and the chaotic, medieval atmosphere of Marrakech. OK, so I adventured so thoroughly I came back with dysentery and had to be hospitalised but I still think solo travel – and I mean *really* solo – is the greatest educator for learning not just about yourself but about life too. It teaches resilience and ingenuity. It teaches you patience and travelling light – have you ever tried hauling a massive suitcase into an airport lavatory cubicle? It reminds you that you can make your own decisions and that sometimes they won't work out but more often than not they will, more or less. It teaches you self-reliance and that is a valuable thing.

I chose to tell you a little about that particular holiday because it wasn't a package trip to Greece where everything is organised for you – although I've done that too, once; that's why I know I don't like it as much as my DIY holidays – and because there is a decided inclination among middle-aged women to allow the walls to close in, to eschew the novel and strange, to scatter a little too much 'oh no, really I couldn't' over life when what we should really be saying is 'bloody hell, yes!' and a lot more often.

It's easy to understand how and why this happens and even easier to allow it to happen to you, to take the path of least resistance. For a start there's more to lose, a bigger stake, with each roll of the non-risk-assessed dice. Sometimes that could be as substantial as a home, possessions, money or a job … or it could be as esoteric as a better understanding of the fragility of health, our own mortality and what we are prepared to put up with, or not.

On the one hand there is an increasing sense of sand trickling ever more quickly through life's hourglass and a desire to seize dangled chances with both hands, but on the other there is trepidation and fear of what the consequences might be should we push the Fates too far (although they are far more forgiving than we might think). This quandary seems to afflict us more at this time in our lives than any other. One reason is undoubtedly that by the time you are middle-aged, life will likely have turned round and bitten you on the bum a few times, which inevitably makes a person more cautious. Although I do wonder if, aside from any practical considerations, one of the things we're most afraid of is embarrassment.

Now, quite possibly this is me projecting my own fears and anxieties on to the issue, but at least that illustrates the agonising process I put myself through before I tackle anything out of the norm. I am still learning the art of spontaneity. I suppose I *could* discuss any tentative plans with friends but I tend not to in case I sound mad or incapable. I certainly won't discuss it with my daughters because they would worry. (This, by the way, is a very good yardstick by which to calculate one's middle-agedness and whether you're doing it right: if your children are worried, a) you *are* middle-aged and b) you *are* doing it right. This is an interesting role reversal and, appealingly, rather like the way I used to behave when I was seventeen.)

There are, of course, an assortment of things that can get in the way of us having a good time on our own and expanding our horizons, knowledge and wisdom through travel, but I'm quite certain that one of the biggest culprits must be that fear of embarrassment. After all, I belong to a generation who would rather get through the whole of life without ever once being embarrassed. I want dignity ... and at the same time I want fun, but the two things seem to be mutually exclusive. The latter implies a certain larky, devil-may-care attitude, which almost certainly results in the loss of the former to some degree.

How to reconcile these conflicting desires? Perhaps we should accept that some slight embarrassment is inevitable and get over ourselves. Alternatively, checking where we think our personal flashpoint lies on embarrassment's sliding scale might help to provide a little perspective. Could you, for instance, take a misunderstanding with a waiter in your stride, or would the arrival at your table of an unexpected and unfortunately all-too-recognisable bovine body part cause you to blush like a cuttlefish? And how are you with 'plumbing'? If faced with a hole in the ground do you beat a hasty retreat? Or perhaps you worry about the absence of proper 'facilities' in the Sahara desert (yes, I have met someone who complained about exactly that) and it stops you taking a two-day guide-led hike? Have you acquired the essential skill of successful solo dining? Would you decide to suffer in silence or improvise rather than mime what you need in an out-of-the-way Greek pharmacy? Can you tactfully disabuse the annoying odd-ball of the idea that because you are on your own you must be The One For Him – even if you are secretly pleased someone still fancies you?

Lack of money is obviously another big inhibitor of middle-aged high jinks. Despite all the media hype about women in this age group having the biggest disposable income, a great many of us live on fairly modest means and sometimes we manage to live on no means at all, just fresh air and worry. Although money is undoubtedly the great shield against life's slings and arrows, I think perhaps that's a bit illusory and it certainly doesn't compensate for a lack of common sense and practical skills. When travelling, for example, money will not protect you from wasp stings, late trains or tummy upsets, but remembering to carry sting relief cream, knowing how to read timetables and manage basic travel hygiene can; and although money can save you a lot of bother with missed connections, excess baggage and whether you can afford to eat or not, so too can sensible planning. If you have money (plenty of it) you can have everything arranged for you and go from home to airport to hotel in a hermetically sealed five-star bubble – but are you getting the most out of the experience? On the basis that you don't have to use your brain, I don't think you are. It sounds very lovely but honestly you might just as well stay at home.

Personally, I find I appreciate a bit of a challenge and an opportunity to test my cunning and ingenuity. Come the zombie apocalypse – and who doesn't worry about that – I will be one of those annoying people with food supplies, a generator and six months' supply of clean knickers. (On the other hand, a four- or five-star hotel with breakfast in your room, on a tray, with a flower in a vase and freshly squeezed orange juice is only one step short of heaven in my opinion. The thing is you can't have it all the time and it quickly becomes boring if you do. Also, and most importantly, you don't learn anything new.)

However, not having much money didn't stop me taking myself to Paris for the first time five years ago. I'd driven around it, I'd flown over it but I'd never actually been *in* it. To be honest, the place terrified me and the fact that it did terrified me even more. I wanted to conquer that fear and be cool and soignée. On a damp November day I boarded the Eurostar and headed for the City of Light. Only it wasn't. It was like every other city in the rain – and it did rain, it rained so much that my trainers became waterlogged and exploded and because I didn't have enough money to replace them I trailed around all day, squelching pathetically up and down grey boulevards because I was also too scared to brave the Métro. I went down and looked at it, decided it was hopeless and came back up again.

I went on the Seine on a tourist boat, in the rain, under an umbrella – apart from a funeral that was the saddest experience of my life. I tried to do the whole day without having to go into a restaurant because I was afraid I wouldn't understand what was being said to me and no one would understand what I was saying to them – a weapons-grade combination of embarrassment and fear together. In the end I buckled somewhere near the Paris Opera and went into a Starbucks where I could point at what I wanted and knew what I would get and could dry out a little in vaguely familiar surroundings.

Yes, it was a miserable day and I totally failed to beat the Parisian terror. I learned plenty, though, and the next time I went I went with a friend who'd lived there for a bit and spoke French. This trip was as delightful as the other had been awful. It was April and the weather was fabulous. We stayed in a little hotel in St Germain and went there from the Gare du Nord in a taxi, which meant I learned how to deal with French cab drivers (not to be underestimated). I asked my friend to show me how the Métro works. We went to a restaurant and I didn't end up with something vile and inedible but instead asked the waiter to deliver my proposal of marriage to the chef who'd made the extraordinary absinthe and hazelnut tart I'd just practically inhaled. (There might have been a glass or two of wine involved there.) Above all it was Fun. The next time I went on my own, again for a day, I once more failed the Métro test (still terrified) but the weather was better and the middle bit of Paris is mostly walkable anyway, and I did manage to go into a shop and successfully buy a blouse so that at least was a step in the right direction.

The Paris breakthrough came when with great kindness I was given a week in a friend's flat in Montmartre in August, when most of the Parisians are themselves away on holiday, which makes the city more tolerable in the same way that London is at that time of year. If you're on your own, self-catering is the only way to go because you have to embrace your temporary home or starve to death. Within a week I had learned supermarket shopping and restaurant ordering and where everything was and that going to the very top of the Eiffel Tower is bowel-looseningly terrifying for anyone afraid of heights (as is coming back down again via the staircase) and I beat the shit out of my biggest fear, hopping gaily on and off the damn Métro for a whole seven days – after an initial fumble or two. In that week I learned to love Paris and it felt like a massive achievement. After all, it took me almost six years.

There is one final point about fear. Something very strange has happened to me over the last couple of years, and other women I meet tell me it's happened to them too. When I left the *Guardian* and went freelance I began to get invitations to speak to an audience and to interview other people. Aside from any self-esteem issues, I was used to being the backroom girl, and it suited me just fine – I was perfectly content tidying up and smoothing everyone else's professional progress. I also suffered from the most crippling stage fright and despite forcing myself to dance on stage, teach and occasionally give a presentation, I'd never in my life managed to conquer it. No one ever had to look far for me before a show – I'd be the one with my head in a bucket backstage, throwing up and shaking violently. Eventually I had to stop doing it because it amounted to self-abuse.

Anyway, when Ari Seth Cohen of the inspiring Advanced Style blog was bringing his crowd-funded documentary to the UK in 2014 I got an email asking if I would be willing to host a Q&A session after the premiere with Ari, Lena (the director) and the Advanced Style ladies. My first thought was that 'Oh no, I couldn't possibly' thought, the one I hate. My second thought was 'Why on earth not?' After all, I'd seen plenty of people host Q&As before, so I ought to know how it was done by now. I was worried about being a short, overweight middle-aged woman up on a stage in front of an audience of about 500 people but how stupid is that when it wasn't me they were coming to see? Why on earth was I worrying about what people thought of *me*? The evening was about Ari, his fabulous film and this group of outstanding older women! And if I didn't do it, what sort of an example was I setting other invisible women like me, especially when I keep yelling from my blog that we should bloody well get out there and be seen?

So I said yes. All evening I had a feeling that something was missing and when I stood up with a microphone in my hand (for the first time ever) I realised what it was – there was a total absence of stage fright. I don't know how to describe the relief when I realised it had gone, that I wasn't shaking, that I didn't feel sick and that I wasn't about to fall off the stage into the front row – except to say that it was like being told that the massive tax bill you thought would bankrupt you belonged to someone else. It was the most fantastically liberating thing and I have no explanation for it.

Since then I've started to be the first one with my hand up in other Q&A sessions – I can't bear that awkward silence while everyone looks at everyone else and nobody dare speak – and who cares if my question's a silly one? I've done a handful of radio interviews (much easier, no audience) and I made my television debut in a BBC documentary about the Bee Gees, which was just delicious and great fun to do. To me it is nothing short of miraculous that there has been not even the smallest sniff of my old enemy, stage fright. I miss it, but only in the way you would miss being punched in the stomach.

The glorious thing is that I'm told this isn't unusual. Apparently it happens because we set a certain amount of personal vanity aside as we age and care far less about what people think of us or expect us to do or be, and we get this dizzying explosion of fearlessness as a sort of consolation prize. And what a prize it is. But I wouldn't want you to go away thinking it's the only prize, because now you know what weapons you have in your armoury you're probably ready to embrace a midlife crisis or three.

4

Pick a crisis

*'If you do not think about your
future, you cannot have one.'*
—John Galsworthy

And so we move on to the dark pleasures of the midlife crisis ...

I'll begin with that familiar but irritating wiggly finger gesture because in my view the term 'midlife crisis' should have inverted commas around it. This is because I am surprised at how little evidence there is that such an apparently common thing even exists and in fact you don't have to go back very far to discover when the term first appeared and who invented it.

In 1965 Dr Elliott Jacques, a Canadian psychoanalyst, wrote a paper for the *International Journal of Psychoanalysis* which he cheerfully titled 'Death and the Mid-Life Crisis'. It contained the following statement:

In the course of the development of the individual there are critical phases which have the character of change points, or periods of rapid transition. Less familiar

> perhaps, though nonetheless real, are the crises which
> occur around the age of thirty-five – which I shall term
> *the mid-life crisis* …

And there it is, the first time the words were used. As far
as facts go that appears to be it: *fact* singular, as opposed
to *facts* plural. Sigmund Freud and Carl Jung wrote quite
a lot about middle age and the unsettling burst of energy
and the hunger for change that usually come with it.
Freud, unsurprisingly, takes a rather negative view and
theorises that it's all to do with death looming towards
us over the horizon, and sex, which also looms and often,
sadly, in the opposite direction. But then that pretty much
describes almost everything Freud wrote so he would say
that, wouldn't he? Altogether more upbeat is Jung and he
describes our midlife mental earthquakes and their attendant aftershocks as the key to individuation. I much prefer
that to Freud – of course I do. To me, becoming more
myself seems not only a more accurate description but also
more logical, appealing, and far less hysterical than the
idea that I should be attempting to cram in as much as
possible before I slip off the dish – although if I'm honest,
there is an element of that too.

In my own middle age I would describe myself as having a pronounced inclination to swing between the quiet
desperation of a doggedly determined person taking on
the world and occasional bouts of furious spitting rage
with sporadic bursts of fierce elation thrown in – all of it
sailing forward on a gentle neap tide of restrained urgency.
I would rationalise this emotional seesaw as due more to

the external pressures I face and my frustration at a world that hasn't caught on to the worth and brilliance of the middle-aged than to any forlorn pursuit of my lost youth. And I say 'neap tide of urgency' because in my experience a sustained gentle(ish) pressure brings much better results than whacking something (or someone?) repeatedly over the head – and of course, as a middle-aged person I stead-fastly refuse to be rushed into anything.

In his 1965 paper Dr Jacques also wrote that 'the tran-sition is often obscured in women by the proximity of the onset of changes connected with the menopause'. This is significant because for a long time men have clasped the midlife crisis to their own hearts and claimed it as theirs alone, which is just a tiny bit dog-in-the-manger-ish of them when the midlife crisis as originally invented – and I hope this chapter will persuade you that it *was* invented – is not entirely gender-specific. We can all have one – or more than one, should we feel inclined.

I am, however, displeased with Dr Jacques for conflat-ing the midlife crisis with symptoms of the menopause because I remember only too well when 'The Change' was considered the go-to excuse for all sorts of slightly wonky behaviour at 'a certain age', from cutting off all your hair and getting a tattoo to a fascination with plumbing – or the plumber … And Christ, all the euphemisms: the cli-macteric, the Big M, the critical period …

As recently as the 1970s middle-aged women caught shoplifting could well find the police let them off because they were at a 'funny age' (there's another one). On one hand, it's delightful to learn I could reinvent myself as

Raffles and blame it all on flitting hormones but on the other, that doesn't half strike me as an outrageously patronising way to treat a woman. Still, that was 50 years ago and we know better now, don't we? Well, no, apparently we don't, or at least not as long as some sections of the media persist in headlines like 'How the menopause can drive women MAD! Panic attacks, depression, hallucinations are just some of the terrifying symptoms you're NOT warned about'. It's almost as though the last 50 years never happened.

I've become more and more resigned to this kind of media treatment. I feel I should keep my powder dry for bigger battles than a minor skirmish over a spot of non-PC stereotyping. Perhaps we'd even be better off allowing the idea that we're all a bit dotty at this age to go unchallenged for a bit to give us some cover while we quietly get on with other more important things. Although it's worth making a bit of a fuss about it and pointing out to anyone who'll listen that this bit of a woman's life is not, in fact, too awful for words because of a few troublesome physical symptoms you may (or may not) have, to a greater or lesser degree.

If anyone was thinking straight then our freshly realigned (by me) middle age of 50 to 65 would be seen as a glorious period of self-affirmation, an invigorating few years of reinvention, evaluation and psychological spring-cleaning – which, let's face it, would be better for everyone. Honestly, sometimes it feels as though achieving the menopause and middle age is rather like joining a secret society because of the negative obfuscation. Consequently it's only when you're in it that you find that

– hurrah! – it was all cobblers, and fully appreciate that at this age you can be beyond magnificent.

Using middle age to replace bits of our psychological IKEA with something more unique and comfortable – more Heal's commissioned, if you like – is something we fall naturally into once we crest 50. In this respect at least, Elliott Jacques was absolutely right to use the word 'crisis'. The root of the word is the Greek *krei-* meaning 'to sieve, discriminate, distinguish'. Out with the old and in with the new – not so much a mental spring clean as an autumnal one. Let a gale or two blow through your remembered life towards your future and see what falls over and what's left standing.

I didn't plan it but that was certainly what I was doing when I was deliberating over what to do and where to go with my life in 2014: I was thinking about which bits I should chuck out and which bits I wanted to keep; what I could live with and what I couldn't. A memory trail of regrets and sorrows, happiness, remorse, pride and defiance led me falteringly through the dusty boxes in my mental attic: some regrets I could fix but while some missed opportunities were gone forever and there was little point in dwelling on them, others emerged as freshly inspiring as the day I'd reluctantly packed them away, offering up the siren song of beginning over again in a life of my choosing. This new, exhilarating life of possibility began to exert the gravitational pull of a small planet and beckoned me towards a future I didn't think I had before I started to think about it. Better still I ... *you* realise that you *can* do it if you really want to.

What I was going through then was undoubtedly a crisis but was it what Freud or Jung or Jacques would recognise as an actual bona fide midlife crisis?

Let's return to our friend Dr Jacques and his positioning of midlife – and the likelihood of an attendant crisis – at around 35 years. This is shocking news, isn't it? I'm quite certain no one thinks of 35 as middle-aged – even less so than the *Oxford English Dictionary*'s 45. It's logical that we keep pegging it back further as we live healthier, more extended lives and I am as sure as you are that 35 is still officially young and not 'midlife' at all. However, when Jacques wrote his 'Death and the Mid-Life Crisis' paper the average life expectancy in the UK was 71.6 years, so in one, very literal sense 35 *was* middle-aged – in 1965. In a more recent article I read that the average age for a midlife crisis is 45, and if you use the same reasoning, that now sounds as though it ought to be about right, when our 2015 average life expectancy is around 85 years. But then I saw yet *another* piece (coincidentally the only one written by a woman) suggesting the whole timeline for midlife needs rewriting anyway because most of our crises happen in our early 50s. At this point my brain began to itch and I gave up. Obviously no one knows. You will have your midlife crisis, if such a thing exists, when circumstances dictate you are ready to have your midlife crisis – then and only then.

Shifting midlife later and later does raise another interesting point though, which is that while we hear a lot about how our ageing population will be a perpetual burden on the young and the State, I wonder whether we will actually spend quite as much time being decrepit and helpless (allegedly) as we will spend in our ever-extending and active *middle age*. We might be older but we're older in better mental and physical health with a superior understanding of how to treat and manage the things that might go wrong. This is worth remembering.

It is, I think, helpful if we take a brief look at what was going on in the couple of years leading up to Professor Jacques's paper because it gives useful context to what might have been orbiting around his thoughts at the time.

In 1965 the culture of youth was gaining real traction, it was a year of significant change in the way age, ageing (and ageing women in particular) were regarded. This was the year that saw the demise of *Vogue*'s Mrs Exeter, after 26 years offering sane and valuable fashion advice to older women. It's hard to imagine *Vogue* having such a column, or making such a statement, in the 21st century, yet when it began in 1949 Mrs Exeter's column was correctly and truthfully illustrated with a photograph of a woman in late middle age. By the time she was retired from the magazine in 1965 the original Mrs Exeter had metamorphosed into a woman in her 30s before even that was considered too old for fashion pages in the Swinging Sixties.

Anyway ... Mrs Exeter was an early victim of 1960s youth culture, which bolted like a new colony of carpet moths and devoured anything and everything associated with fusty middle age until it reached the point where we are now: threadbare and sorry-looking. I freely admit that I thoroughly enjoyed the 'Youthquake' while I was in it, but as mentioned earlier, it never occurred to any of us to think about what might happen once we were through it and out the other side. We kicked off that second wave of feminism and then we ran out of steam before we could think about what comes next – although, in the spirit of middle age 'sifting', I don't think we should be too hard on ourselves: there's still time to set things straight.

Reading back through newspapers from the mid-60s reminds me how differing attitudes created conflict between the generations off the back of the widening cultural divide – as in 1964 when the Beatles began their American tour and we saw the birth of 'Beatlemania'. As a very junior Beatles fan I remember spending my pocket money on the new special packs of bubble gum to collect Fab Four fan cards and I had a black plastic 'guitar' brooch with a picture of Paul in it. As a child I was as completely bewildered by all the shrieking, screaming and hysteria that I saw on the television news as my parents were. What was *that* all about? At nine years old, pop stars came fourth on my list of great loves, after Malory Towers, prima ballerinas and ponies.

Mum and dad must have been immensely relieved when I completely failed to clock another aftershock from the Youthquake with the appearance of pirate radio – Radios Caroline, Atlanta and Sutch all began broadcasting offshore in '64. And I was certainly far too young to appreciate the significance of Helen Brook establishing the first Brook Advisory Centre – that came much later. I asked my mum to buy me the new *Jackie* magazine, although she declined on the grounds that it was too progressive and modern (actually I think she just declined and no grounds were mentioned). Revisiting the pages of *Jackie* in recent years and the 'Cathy and Claire' problem page in particular, I begin to understand my parents' reluctance – to them all that advice about bodies, boys and kissing (in among plenty of other, more mundane stuff) must have looked like complete degeneracy. In fact at times the country looked as though it would descend into all-out intergenerational war. When the Mods and Rockers' running battles along the South Coast sparked moral panic, mum and dad must have wondered where on earth it would all end.

Paddling about in these warm waves of nostalgia I came across two newspaper clippings from the *Daily Telegraph* that for me seem to sum up the middle-aged woman of the 1960s – courageous, resourceful and respected but also slightly irrelevant. The first was a reference to the election of Harold Wilson as Prime Minister, speculating on what it must have been like for Mrs Wilson, Mary, to move into Downing Street: 'At No. 10 Mrs Wilson will undoubtedly appreciate the kitchens.' And that was all they had to say on the matter. The kitchen was the woman's place 50 years ago, even at the heart of government. Disappointingly, an analysis of the No. 10 kitchens and décor continues to provide the mainstay for present-day media who can think of nothing more interesting to say about a Prime Minister's wife, even though the 21st century version is very likely to be a professional woman in her own right. (Samantha Cameron is apparently 'known for her love of slick Scandi-style chic', never mind having been a director of Smythson's of Bond Street.) So not much has changed there then.

The second piece to catch my eye concerned a Mrs Stott, a Mrs Green and the Mods of Margate. The *Telegraph* reports that

> Mrs Lily Stott, 53, manageress [of the Margate station buffet], a small grey-haired woman wearing spectacles, was thrown to the ground by one Mod. Two others dragged her face down around the floor.

But do not fear, for

> Mrs Ellen Green, 50, a cleaner, emerged with a broom and started laying about her to assist Mrs Stott. Mrs Green said: 'I caught hold of one girl by the hair and dealt with her.' She chased two youths out through the booking office and held one until the police arrived.

Here we have two middle-aged women, but most especially Mrs Green, emerging from a dreadful experience, battered but undefeated. However, at the grand old age of 53 Mrs Stott is described as 'small' and 'grey-haired' – like a little old lady. How many 53-year-olds these days could be described like that? History does not record the physical stature of Mrs Green but I imagine Boudicca in a wrap-over pinny and a pair of Marigolds.

To me, the story of Mrs Green and Mrs Stott illustrates how differently we regard women in their 50s now, both physically and temperamentally. Stories about a 'have a go granny' tackling a mugger crop up with reasonable frequency but are restricted to the more traditional type of granny (elderly, infirm and riding a mobility scooter), rather than the more capable sort of middle-aged granny of which there are so many. There doesn't seem space for the everyday kind of heroism engaged in by the middle-aged woman living in today's equally hostile environment, except when they're doing something classically 'midlife crisis' daft.

The following year, in 1965 – the year that saw the birth of the midlife crisis – the Beatles film *Help!* had its debut in London; the word 'fuck' premiered on British television courtesy of theatre critic Kenneth Tynan; and, I speculate partly as a response to this, Mary Whitehouse founded the National Viewers' and Listeners' Association – she was 54 and with her hats and horn-rims perfectly fits what was then, and now, regarded as the archetypal middle-aged woman. Possibly, aside from her somewhat puritanical views (by today's standards), this is why she was often seen as something of a joke and lampooned accordingly.

Also in 1965, Mary Quant introduced the miniskirt from her shop, Bazaar, on London's King's Road, and this, in my view, marked more of a turning point for the middle-aged woman than any of the other more dramatic developments of the time.

It's easy to overlook the way fashion shapes how we think – it appears such a trivial, ephemeral thing – but it shouldn't be forgotten that up until the mid-60s 'the young' mostly dressed like their parents. In 1965, small girls of ten were miniature versions of their mothers. I clearly remember my little group going about in twinsets as part of a traditional ensemble including either a sensible skirt or stretch stirrup pants, our hair sensibly cut and curled with rags (home-grown torture) or those curling tongs you heated on the cooker. Despite my tomboy inclinations, I remember thinking it a tremendous treat to be taken for tea and cakes in town, and for this I would be dressed up: patent shoes, white socks, gloves, smart frock, hat and a mustard-coloured double-breasted coat with brass and pearl buttons and fur collar: a mini-grown-up in every respect bar the socks. My mum's lessons in etiquette are the only reason I ever achieved full mastery over the vanilla slice. I am proud of this.

Whenever you went to a birthday party in the mid-60s you went in your old bridesmaid dress: mine was pale lemon and frilly with a posy of silk flowers and ribbons at the waist; my best friend's was similar but a tangerine colour and it had a bolero. Indeed there were so many frilly little girls that if you tripped over during an energetic bout of musical chairs you ran the risk of suffocation.

My fashion epiphany came at around the age of twelve, at a party where the young hostess appeared, fashionably late, as a vision in black velvet miniskirt and matching waistcoat (gold chain fastening) worn over a white frilled blouse. Not only that but she'd been to an *actual* Beatles concert and she had their *actual* autographs!

In the wider world outside little girls' tea parties, this was when the miniskirt became mainstream, when the fashion compass swung in the opposite direction and ushered in a decades-long outlawing of the fashionable older woman. There was no way a middle-aged knee could measure up in a miniskirt. Older women attempting the new fashions were termed 'mutton dressed as lamb' and there was a dividing of the sartorial ways. We became what we wore – the young were very much 'in' with their short hemlines and five-point bobs while a lower hemline and a perm identified the middle-aged as very much 'out'. For them, behaving 'young' became the hallmark of a classic midlife crisis.

Isn't it a cruel irony that the very moment Mrs Exeter's tumbril trundled off the pages of *Vogue* towards the guillotine was the very moment when we needed her most? There is a die-hard group of Mrs Exeter enthusiasts (I am one) who from time to time have a go at getting her reinstated but since a piece in the *Daily Mail* in 2006, Alexandra Shulman, *Vogue*'s editor, has refused to be drawn further on the subject:

> Those old enough to remember Mrs Exeter often write to me to ask whether we could bring her back to life. Apart from having limited powers of resuscitation, I am not bringing her back to the pages of *Vogue* because Mrs Exeter nowadays would simply not work as an idea.
>
> Far from wanting their own fashion commentator, most women over 50 do not wish to be thought of as living in a different shopping and dressing cosmos to the rest of the world. What we want is for the rest of the world to take into account our particular requirements.

Yes, and we're still waiting. So in the meantime, while the rest of the world gets round to it, would it be too much to ask that we women over 50 have some advice about how we adapt clothes designed and made to fit fifteen-year-old 000 size models so that we don't look like a laughing stock? Far from being democratic, fashion is the worst ageist offender of all. *Vogue* and the rest of the glossy magazine sisterhood continue to enjoy a party to which we 50- to 65-year-olds are not invited.

Turning to another (alleged) hallmark of an (alleged) midlife crisis, are we really visited by a sudden realisation that there is more of life behind than before us? Elliott Jacques called his 1965 paper 'Death and the Mid-life Crisis' because that moment, if we have it, gives us the biggest shove down the primrose path towards the mirage of eternal youth. I think most people will have come to terms with the faintly surprising news that with every birthday we grow a little older long before this kind of psychological lightning strike. Of course that doesn't mean that we won't at least try to hang on to some of the certainty and comfort we had when we were 30, when we knew where we were and what we were doing here. We crave the security and purpose of our old routine – it was a lot more comfortable than the vagueness and uncertainty that accompanies the stretch preceding old age. So, it isn't necessarily literal death that kicks us down this cul-de-sac but the death of one way of life to make way for another (which is why the midlife milestone of retirement is often cited as another trigger for a crisis – the fact that it keeps receding might actually help us in this respect).

It's the same process we went through when we were teenagers only then we couldn't wait to transform into adults with all their attendant freedoms, including a licence to fuck up and oodles of time to fuck up in. This transformation is the other way around – we're reluctant to let go of the past because once we do it might feel like we've taken an irretrievable step into an alternative existence where there is no time left to do anything but mourn the death of dreams. Dear lord … I blame Freud for this one.

Forget about navel-gazing and set your mind to the task of understanding that the whole business is less about death and the end of life than about coming into your own, properly. Just as you had to experiment with finding out who you were when you went from being a teenager to an adult, you're going to do it all again now, only this time you're going from adult to *super*-adult. That sounds a bit New Age-y but what I'm trying to say is that it's really not about losing things in a downward slide, it's about building on what you have with all your knowledge and experience to help you do it.

> '*Death is the last enemy: once we've got past*
> *that I think everything will be alright.*'
> —ALICE THOMAS ELLIS

Now that I've mentioned the D-word and its connections to midlife crises it's worth talking about it a bit because like everything else we try to avoid, its scare value lies in that very fact. We won't discuss it, we don't think about it, we make no attempt to understand our feelings about it and consequently it scares the bejesus out of us. Just a minute though ... didn't we feel the same way about middle age before we found out that it's really rather nice? I wouldn't go so far as to say that facing the Grim Reaper is in any way 'nice' but as one of my close friends said, shortly before she kept her own appointment with the man with the scythe, 'it is what it is'. I believe it's as well to reconcile that fact in your own mind rather than suddenly think to yourself: 'What, *now*? But I've got yoga at eleven o'clock ...'

I confess I used to be really very afraid of death, especially in the grip of my 2003 cancer scare – it can appear so random and unfair. At the time I often thought about one of the last things my mother said: 'There was so much I wanted to do'. I still think about that now. In all honesty I don't think there can be many of us who, on reaching our final moments, don't think that – we will always regret what we haven't done, the things we passed up because we were too timid or too busy.

In the gap between my diagnosis and post-op test results, when it crossed my own mind (roughly every ten minutes) that I might not make it, a friend recommended I read *Mort*, a book from Sir Terry Pratchett's Discworld series. I'd always avoided these books because they seemed to shriek 'GEEK', which makes me the worst kind of intellectual snob. In fact what Pratchett's books *are* is intelligent, witty and screamingly funny analyses of the human condition. After reading *Mort* I enthusiastically embraced my inner geek and romped through the entire series over my months of recuperation. Pratchett's invention of Death as a dignified, cat-loving deliverer of gin-dry aperçus, inspiring respect as he harvests souls, provided me with an opportunity to see a human, funny side to what frightened me. It also gave me an appetite to explore further and Diana Athill's advice about taking a few minutes each day to think about and come to terms with it (not in any morbid sense) is the most grounded and sensible thing I think I've ever heard. Getting myself familiar with this most basic fear, strangely, brought a sense of blessed relief.

Coming to terms with our own mortality might help banish personal terrors but what of our loss and grief in the aftermath of the death we face most often in our middle years – that of our parents? It might also be the first time we lose a friend, someone who is the same age as we are, and it would be surprising if we sailed through without hitting the buffers over this one. Ironically, being prepared doesn't seem to prepare you. I only realised that fairly recently because it took me far too long, a lifetime in fact, to work it out.

The first time I encountered the death of someone I knew was at primary school when a schoolmate developed leukaemia. I remember a special school assembly, I remember her name and what she looked like and I remember feeling confused. Children did not die.

The next loss was closer to home when my mother's mother died of stomach cancer. That my mum had lost *her* mum threw me into a panic. That my mum might die was the worst thing I could ever imagine happening to me. This ushered in my 'God' phase. My mum was very churchy but I think even she found a fervently pious ten-year-old a bit much to cope with. I rounded that stage off by winning the school cup for Religious Knowledge, the only school prize I ever won in my life. And then I seemed to get over it.

In hindsight, it's probably a good thing I did that early working out of where I stood spiritually because my mum *did* die. Of course she did, we all do; but mothers are not supposed to die when their daughters are 20 and newly married. Whenever I look back over my life I fall into thinking of BM and AM – Before Mum and After Mum. The grief and anger I felt at the time was entirely normal but I hadn't, and wasn't, prepared for the violence of it. Because mum's tussle with colon cancer had been long and arduous and because we knew the outcome was inevitable almost from the beginning I thought I would cope, that the moment it happened was just another step along the way. Between her death and the day of the funeral all I felt was relief and gladness that she was no longer suffering. Grief and shock hit me head-on the very second I set eyes on the coffin, in a hearse outside our house. I think I lost myself for about eighteen months. Perhaps the only person who could have guided me through it was the one in the box. My family splintered apart and it took a very long time for us to mend ourselves.

I gave up post-event regrets when I turned 50 (a conscious decision) but before I could do that I had to hack through a painful thicket of them that thrived around mum. Remorse and wanting to put right past mistakes is, I discover, another trigger for a midlife crisis but these feelings are not exclusive to middle age; they are the same feelings that go with every major life change, most especially when one thing ends painfully so that another can begin. Every other thought seems to begin 'I wish I had …' and I wish I had learned that before I lost mum. I wish I hadn't been such a horrible stroppy teenager. I wish I'd been around more before she got ill. I wish she'd seen her grandchildren and great-grandchildren. I wish she could have seen the woman I've become. Although she would certainly have disapproved of many of the things I've done, I like to think … no, I *wish* she could have been proud of me. I wish I hadn't wasted so much time tying myself in knots while I tried to second-guess and work things out. And what can we hope to achieve by it, this bleakly painful search for self-absolution? Some of us do it for years. I wish … I wish … I wish …

The only word that describes the time after close personal loss is 'cold'. For me, it was a world of hurt and it seemed as though all the love was gone. You should learn from this experience and store up that knowledge for the next time – because there *will* be a next time.

You're officially an adult at 21 and you certainly think you are but I went off like a defective firework after mum died: I drank too much, smoked too much, screwed up my job, took drugs, had an affair and afterwards I ran off to France … I did everything I could to fill the vacuum, only nothing ever did, or could. Eventually I came out of it, surprisingly still married, and a year later I was pregnant with my first child.

The next time I experienced howling grief was fifteen years later with the death of my marriage in a divorce that was not only messy, complicated, harrowing and hateful but also, initially, separated me from my children. Starting again in these circumstances is like being told to run a marathon with a broken leg. Predictably and for about six months I did exactly what I'd done when mum died. What was it Einstein said about that? Oh yes, 'Insanity is doing the same thing over and over again and expecting different results'. I was 35 when all that happened and borderline for the Elliott Jacques definition of a midlife crisis. It wasn't that though, it was just a crisis – a life crisis of a kind that is fairly commonplace. Eventually I picked myself up, found my courage and somewhere to live, got a job and then successfully fought through the courts to get my children back. I started again.

I bet you're ahead of me now and, yes, of course, it happened again – when I was 45, again triggered by death. This time it was a year's worth of car accidents that wrecked its way through our circle of friends. For twelve months I seemed to spend my days ferrying teenagers to visit people in hospital or propping them up at funerals. You wouldn't need to be a head doctor to work out how I reacted to all of that. I did the whole 'firework' trick again but I did eventually finish up moving to London, which was at least constructive and useful. At 45 I was certainly approaching middle age but was all of that a midlife crisis? I don't think so. The only thing I had any control over was changing location. I wonder if control and retaining could be the key?

By the time I hit the next bout of bereavements (why do these things always come in batches?) I had succeeded in working out that my selfish and self-destructive derailing post-mortem was a kind of reflex. I decided I couldn't face doing all that again. So, through the loss of my father, my stepmother, two good friends and my beloved cat, I managed to maintain my composure and retain control, of myself at least. I'd learned, finally, that there's nothing to be gained and it helps no one to rage against the junk life throws at you. I've learned to roll with the punches and while I might not always leap straight back up again, I have managed, every time, to get myself more or less upright eventually. There have been times over the last two years (the toughest I can remember) when I honestly thought I was done for but with a degree of resignation I managed to hold my course, steer more or less straight and eventually I got through it. Battered and bowed but definitely not broken, I think, finally, I've made it to grown-up.

Was *that* my midlife crisis?

Surely one of these must count? But again, although it was undoubtedly a crisis – or a series of crises – that happened in midlife they were, all of them, again driven by external factors. I had no control over any of it, except the way I coped with each situation that came along. In any case I think it's trite to sweep a whole load of complicated psychological and physical issues into one bucket. You can't just slap on a label and dismiss it. Whether you believe in the midlife crisis or not, it's just plain wrong to make assumptions just because there's a convenient peg to hang things on. Midlife is much more important than that. The knocks and setbacks we experience, the forgotten yearnings that resurface, encouraging us to instigate life changes that are probably long overdue, force us to get off our backsides instead of coasting through what should be a productive, enjoyable few years and wasting them. And if we're going to do something rather than nothing then we're only going to go one of two ways: either we decide to go back to something we've always longed to return to, or we try something we've never tried before but have always wanted to try. Or perhaps we arrive at a satisfying combination of the two ... which makes three ways, sorry. Whatever. But we do need to do something for ourselves and it's nearly always something that those who don't understand the condition might see as 'selfish'.

If, in all the exhausting catalogue of films on the subject, there is one bit of dialogue that precisely sums up the midlife state of mind, then it has to be two of the lines spoken by Kevin Spacey's character, Lester Burnham, in *American Beauty*: 'It's a great thing when you realise you still have the ability to surprise yourself. Makes you wonder what else you can do that you've forgotten about.' What he's describing is the sort of midlife revelation so many of us experience when we start sifting our experiences and desires, the one which shows us that despite being consigned to the 'boring and coasting into retirement' demographic by younger colleagues/the boss/your children/neighbours/the advertising industry and falling into the trap of half-believing it, you *do* still have a life ahead of you that means something. The problem comes in the way everyone else projects their own expectations on to that and because you're not behaving according to the accepted standard (in their opinion) you have obviously gone mad. Or you're having a midlife crisis – a label invented to cover all such eventualities so that no one has to think about it too hard.

When I listen to Lester's monologues they constantly nudge me towards considering how I would answer those questions myself, in my own life. 'I had my whole life ahead of me,' he says, wistfully, and sets about recreating his life as it was when he felt he was happiest – with fewer responsibilities, more opportunity and the possibility and promise of not being hemmed in by what everyone else wants or expects. I don't think any of us seriously want to be 21 again but what we *do* want is that feeling of having it all to discover, of standing on the threshold of a lifetime of adventures. If you start believing what we're encouraged to believe, that it's all over bar the shouting, then I reckon you're done for. And anyway, it isn't … not by a long way.

A better interpretation of 'midlife crisis' is surely 'midlife reminder'. Middle age is a reminder that here is a period in our lives when we should be getting on with things and tidying up the trailing loose ends of unfulfilled dreams and ambitions. When we hit this evolutionary pause for thought it's only natural to look back at what we did well and how happy we were doing it. The next thing we think about is probably whether we'd go back to doing those things again. What's interesting about this is that most measure this past happiness not by *what* it was they were doing but by *how old they were* when they were doing it, which is the wrong way round. The age part of that scenario is irrelevant.

Now consider this: 50 years ago (before Elliott Jacques) middle age and retirement were something to be looked forward to, prepared for and enjoyed. Ordinary lives then were time poor and labour intensive; foreign travel was still expensive and life was mostly lived in the same place. Retirement offered an opportunity for a well-earned rest doing more of the things we enjoyed – a reward for a lifetime's toil. Our expectations were modest. Those of us at that point today have grown up in a thrusting, materialistic, youth-centric society – in fact we added a fair amount to that ourselves – and we have had far more opportunity, cash and free time to do what we wanted to do, when we wanted to do it: retirement could well signal the end of all that and be seen as a punishment for growing old, as a banishment from the mainstream. Our expectations are *not* modest and we want more of the same. We know only that to be young is to be with the in crowd; to be middle-aged or, God forbid, *old* is to be with the out crowd. The middle-aged are a constant reminder that staying with the in crowd forever is not going to be an option and at some point you will find yourself cast out into the wilderness – a bit like the film *Logan's Run* but not quite so drastic.

With a little foresight in the past we might have avoided this but there you go and for the time being we're stuck with it, although somehow and on top of all that we appear to have put the young in charge of everything, which I think can only be seen as a fairly major tactical error on our part. It's quite obvious that somehow we need to redress the balance. I'm not talking about starting a fight over it – there's quite enough intergenerational provocation going on already – but can't we just have a little bit of acknowledgement that we haven't made it this far without hardship, learning our life lessons and accumulating wisdom? Instead of finding our opportunities shutting down we should see them opening up so that rewarding ourselves for all the effort by making our own choices about how we choose to live from now on becomes less of a battle with everyone else. If that means changing the way we live our lives to make us happier then we should be able to do that without those actions being interpreted as a supposed 'midlife crisis', which in turn has come to mean that we are not to be taken seriously because quite obviously we're experiencing a temporary glitch in our antiquated 'sanity' wiring. We are actually engaged in difficult and important work on our own behalf and we've never felt *more* sane.

5

Trivial pursuits?

> *'See, what you're meant to do when you have a
> midlife crisis is buy a fast car, aren't you? Well
> I've always had fast cars. It's not that. It's the fear
> that you're past your best. It's the fear that the
> stuff you've done in the past is your best work.'*
> —ROBBIE COLTRANE

Thank goodness I never gave in to parental pressure
and killed off that inconvenient habit (inconvenient
to them, not me) of refusing to take no for an answer. I
found being in the so-called Awkward Squad helped give
me a distinct advantage in my adult life, especially career-
wise and most particularly when I got to the more ... *senior*
part of that. Occasionally dignified, tactical surrender is
called for but it's usually much more in my best interests
to stick to my guns until I've weighed up what's what and
decided whether 'no' is in fact the right answer for me.
If I decide it's not then I keep coming at a problem from
up, down and sideways until I've either a) got around it
or b) proved conclusively and beyond all doubt that I'm
beaten. The outcome was rarely b). There was almost

always another way and I kept telling myself that in 2014 when I was out of work and stuck, more stuck than I'd ever been.

When you start to wobble, the fear Robbie Coltrane talks about in the above quote, of worrying that your best years might be behind you, is as pervasive as cat hair. It gets into everything you do – it underpins every thought you have. It's another damn thing to fight and tempting though it is to lie down and let the world and its wife walk all over you, you must not give in. If you give in then you're condemning yourself to accepting second best, perhaps even third or fourth best. It's your life and you can't afford to do that. None of us can. Here's why ...

The Commission on Older Women Interim Report (2013) found that 'women in their fifties face the widest pay gap of any age group'. As mentioned earlier in the book, the Commission also found that 'unemployment amongst women aged 50–64 has increased by a staggering 41 per cent ... compared with one per cent overall'. In apparent contradiction to that the report also states, 'employment levels amongst women in their fifties and sixties have been on the rise'. Surely that's not possible? Well, in the wonderful and perplexing world of 'lies, damn lies and statistics' I'm afraid it is, because while falling unemployment figures have been much trumpeted by the UK's coalition government, 85 per cent of that reported growth in our middle-aged employment rate is down to the ever-receding state pension age. What this means is that we must hang on to our jobs and stay in work for longer or we run the risk of depleting whatever savings we have managed to squirrel away just to keep ourselves going – and should you find yourself out of work at 60 then you must move heaven, earth and age-biased employers to find yourself another job for the same reason.

As for the gender pay gap, as it currently stands, women over the age of 50 and working full-time earn an average of 18 per cent less than their male counterparts; if you needed any further convincing, that's *twice* as large as the pay gap for women overall. If you feel strong enough to take that statistic further you'll find it also paints a deeply gloomy picture of our pension entitlements because any gaps and deficits in our working lives show up very clearly in whatever pension pot we've managed to scrape together during our working lives. Remember before April 1977, when you could choose to opt in or out of a reduced rate of National Insurance for married women? You may well find that relying on the state pension won't be quite the lifeline you thought it was if you opted to stay in. The same thing applies if you decided, as many of us did, to drop out of work altogether to bring up a family. Then there's the rising divorce rate ...

You don't have to take my word for it – you could read the report by UNISON, 'Women Deserve Better' (2014), which shows there is an average '30 per cent pensions gap for women relative to men'. Another paper, 'The Gender Gap in Pensions in the EU', by the European Commission (2013), puts the UK figure even higher at 43 per cent – the third highest level in the EU, behind Luxembourg and Germany. Worse still is that 37 per cent of women in the UK have no pension at all and 'many expect to rely on their partner's retirement income, leaving them vulnerable on divorce or separation'. Short of posting it on top of the Houses of Parliament in 20-foot letters of fire I really can't make it any clearer. We need to work.

The problem is that in your sixth decade not only are you battling against your own apparent invisibility but you're taking on the faceless, invisible forces that keep you there: ageism and sexism … sexist ageism … ageist sexism … they're all the same combination of the same toxic prejudicial fog and they're slippery feckers.

We are a fighting generation of women. We fought for better employment rights, childcare and equal pay and we fought against sexism and objectification and as such I don't have a problem using whatever platform is available to draw attention to some of those same difficulties we're facing now. In fact, the miracle of the Internet means we *all* have a platform – that's one of the things that blogging, vlogging and social media have done for us. I couldn't quite work out the point of it either when I began but now I honestly don't know why more of us aren't at it. Given the difficulty placing an article telling the plain, unvarnished truth about what middle age means for most women ('we were looking for something more … *positive*?'), rather than the idealised, sun-dappled, relentlessly upbeat picture of wine and river cruises thrust at us from most media, it's not only a good way but possibly the *only* way we have of waving a flag, planting it and shouting 'Hey! We're still here!'

Being visible on the Internet would perhaps help us to debunk one of the more popular myths about the middle-aged: the one that has us all down as fumbling, hopeless IT illiterates. There are a few – of course there are – but by and large we are on top of our game with this. In the early 1990s when I first began working in the determinedly uncool Department of Medicine for the Elderly, we medical secretaries were all bashing out the patients' clinic and discharge letters on electric typewriters, in triplicate. We were not allowed to correct things; if we made a mistake we had to start again. You can imagine the waste and frustration (although on the other hand I did become deadly accurate).

I remember the day we were all summoned for a computer demonstration, which was followed up with the tentative suggestion that this might be The Future. I also remember what I said that day: I said, 'I'm not working on one of *those*.' I blush to think of it now but it wasn't just me, none of us thought it would catch on and anyway none of us liked the idea of changing so we dug in our Luddite heels. But you can't stand in the way of technological change. Any protests were swept aside by the management and a couple of years further on I'd embraced both change and computers to the extent that I owned one of these terrifying things, allowing me to work from home as a freelance medical secretary instead of being based at the hospital as I had previously. I also used it to carry on running the design business I'd started from home in the late '80s, before my divorce; I wrote copy for theatre programmes on it and my daughters did their homework on it. These self-taught/self-starter skills were what helped land me my first job in London.

I had learned that keeping your mind open and curious is one of the most vital things you will ever do, and you must never stop doing it because nothing will ever stay the same. It's not always immediately apparent how any new thing might benefit you personally but sometimes chance lands you both in the right place and at very much the right time to use it, whatever *it* is. I offer you the following illustration.

Bagging that job at the *Guardian* when I did was one of the best things I could have done at that particular point in my life. (I say, 'bag' but it took no fewer than five interviews and a 150-question psychometric test to secure it.) Any niggling middle-aged fears I might have had about computers and how they worked evaporated after a couple of months of working for someone in the grip not of techno fear but techno *joy*. I had to switch from working with a PC to working with a Mac, which involved forgetting the last ten years spent learning to use the former and being mildly confounded by the latter but finishing up as a sort of computer bilingual – a useful thing to be – and every so often the editor would leave A Thing on my desk with an instruction to find out what the Thing did and whether it might be in any way useful to us.

Learning all this stuff is as stimulating as it is easy and, at the point you 'get' it, a bit like applying jump leads to your brain as possibilities balloon up in your imagination. It just means spending a bit of time fiddling and constantly reminding yourself that it's almost impossible to actually, physically break anything (unless frustration provokes you into chucking it out of a window). It could also bring you opportunities to do things that you'd never thought about before. Like this conversation I had with my boss one Friday afternoon inside the old Guardian Towers on Farringdon Road.

Boss: 'What are you up to at the weekend?'

Me: 'Nothing much … reading. Might meet a friend for coffee.'

Boss: 'Why don't you make a film?'

Me: 'What? I wouldn't know where to start.'

Boss: 'You could set your little camera to "video" and film things and then on Monday morning I'll show you how to edit it.'

Me (pulling best sceptical face): 'I'll think about it.'

In the event, I did take my little camera out and I filmed my feet walking around South-East London; occasionally I flipped the camera upwards to show where I was (Canary Wharf, Blackheath, Greenwich Park). It gave me roughly five minutes' worth of amateur video.

On Monday morning:

Boss: 'Did you film anything?'

Me (typical girl response): 'Yup. It's not very good. What do I do with it?'

I uploaded my little bit of film from the camera to my office Mac and then I was on my own because when my boss had said he'd show me how to edit my film that was actually a fib and he had no more idea than I did. It took me a couple more days of mucking about with it before I could post the finished product on Facebook, soundtrack and all.

I completely understand this was me acting in the role of the editor's tech guinea pig at a time when video journalism was very much the coming thing. He wanted to see how easy it was and if his PA could do it ... It would have been the simplest thing in the world to get all prickly over this mildly patronising (but unvoiced) experiment but I'm glad I didn't because then I wouldn't have started up a whole new offshoot to my career. The original Facebook film brought me a commission to produce a promo film for a classical CD, which went to the New York offices of the record label and started me off on a nice little creative detour. It changed the way I built visual presentations. I made showreels of *Guardian* journalism with punchy soundtracks, I filmed second camera with a film unit and I had a tremendous amount of fun.

Where it all came from I have no idea but it was *thrilling* to discover this new skill. I'd been put off photography because in the past I'd always got it wrong. In those days, of course, it was film photography but with digital photography, where you see what you're doing on a little screen before you do it – well, that solved the problem with my astigmatism and a whole new creative world opened up for me. This is what I meant when I quoted Lester's line from *American Beauty* in the previous chapter – it *is* a great thing to surprise, not just yourself, but everyone else as well. We all have that ability to ignite a latent talent. The opportunity doesn't always land in our laps in the way that one did but perhaps we forget that we can sometimes nudge them along and create them out of very little. The best opportunities often come out of something we took a chance on, or thought 'I wouldn't mind having a go at that'. Don't be afraid and don't be discouraged.

When I think of the list of things I've been put off or afraid to try in the past I could be feeling very sad and angry. I'm giving it a go now though, for myself as much as anyone and no, it's *not* a midlife crisis (I think we've established that). I remember being made to stand for an hour in a French lesson because shyness prevented me from singing a verse from a song in front of the whole class. Somehow the experience stopped me speaking any French or singing at all for many years. The speaking French bit I sorted out quite quickly once I started travelling but I only started properly getting to grips with the singing part a couple of years ago. That I can't carry a tune in a bucket doesn't matter one iota – the pleasure I get from belting out a song in the kitchen is possibly the best mood enhancer I know (aside from a single malt).

To return to technology ... even ten years ago, it was mostly the practice that employers would forbid the use of social media during working hours but at the *Guardian* we were encouraged to get in there, to experiment. I am grateful for this too, especially now that the world apparently runs on Twitter, which I find particularly useful for all sorts of things. Watching how quickly news spreads continues to fascinate me. A thousand thoughts and actions can spring from one very small idea or just a handful of words – although not always in a good way (it gives a whole new dimension to the saying that 'a lie can travel halfway around the world while the truth is putting on its shoes'). If you've never taken the time to look at how far one of your tweets travels then I urge you to try it. When I began writing my *Guardian* column I could track how far I reached by following the tweets like a trail of breadcrumbs and it was one of the things that gave me the encouragement to continue – that, and the reader responses to what I'd written. It was truly staggering when I saw the first hashtag on my global tweet map open, proliferate and then seed itself from continent to continent, lapping the globe in a matter of minutes. To see your words racing away at the speed of light is a useful reminder that social media, although undoubtedly fun, is also extremely powerful. It has toppled governments, caused politicians to resign and ruined careers, in 140 characters or fewer. Handle it as you would a live firework.

On a more personal level, being able to source information about somewhere new by posting a few questions to your network of followers before you step off a train can be a great time saver. In the working day it can help with inspiration, as it did when I visited the *Vogue* Festival, anonymously but under the *Guardian* label, which can be the only reason their PR collared me as I walked through the door and invited me to interview Dolce & Gabbana. I'd never interviewed anyone in my life. My colleagues on the fashion desk would never have forgiven me if I'd said no to that but I only had 20 minutes to prepare and my head was so empty of facts that any thoughts wandering in looked around and left again very quickly. This is what panic does to you – I had 'But I'm only some bloke's PA' replaying on a loop over and over again. I went for what my inebriate aunt would have called 'a stiffener' (a top use of what little time I had) and from my seat at the bar I tweeted a question to my little band of Twitter followers.

What would you ask Dolce & Gabbana if you were in my shoes?
I asked. Amazingly a handful of decent questions came
back. My subjects looked a little surprised when I asked
them what their favourite chocolate was but I'd already
'fessed up that I was a novice at this. They were kind and
lovely and had worked together for so long they finished
each other's sentences, and somehow I got my interview …
and then I went and had another drink to celebrate.

Because I said yes instead of no – or more truthfully
because I'd been too scared to say no instead of yes – I'd
done something that terrified me and achieved something
in spite of myself. How often in my life have I said 'Oh
no, I couldn't possibly'? To think about it would be too
depressing.

Fiddling about on social media didn't stop once I'd left
the *Guardian* but it did change. The way I used it became
more personalised and more a way of keeping up with
what was relevant to my future plans. I used it to build a
network of like-minded people. It solves the problem of
where you find other people like yourself to 'talk' to when
you live alone.

For me personally, social media has really come into its
own over the past couple of years, because as my real-life
social universe shrank my virtual one grew and became
a vital contact with an outside world I often didn't feel
like facing. Through all that long dark night of the soul,
when I was looking for work and coping with one bereavement after another, there were days when I felt as though
I was barely functioning, when I could hardly work out
which way was up. Social media generally, and Twitter in

particular, opened up my life when everything else seemed to be closing down. It felt rather like having friends round for a drink but with no washing up and no requirement to change my clothes or put some slap on. Even in the middle of a dismal night in a hotel when you've got one ear cocked for a call from the hospice, there is someone awake somewhere in the world who will talk to you about ordinary things and make life feel normal again. I don't feel it's necessary to spill your emotional guts out on to your Twitter feed (where it might come back like last night's kebab) but just saying that you're struggling a bit or asking if anyone else is going through x, y or z frequently brings you a ton of virtual support just when you need it.

As far as the famous Internet trolls go, I have so far (fingers crossed) managed to get off lightly, although I don't doubt I'll get it in the neck eventually, simply for being an older woman with the effrontery to be 'out' in the first place. On the odd occasion when I have been on the receiving end of some unpleasantness I've done what other, more experienced users like Mary Beard have done and sent the message out to my followers, who will offer support or possibly wade in on my behalf. But as a rule I try not to get drawn into a row – after all, it's not compulsory to reply to everything. It's also worth remembering that, as is the way with text messaging, the briefer the written word the more it can be open to misinterpretation – tweets don't translate well to sarcasm or irony and I don't mind saying I'm sorry if I've upset someone. To quote my mum (with a minor adjustment), 'If you haven't got anything nice to tweet then don't tweet anything at all'. Mind you, she was also given to saying 'Little birds in their nests agree' – and I've no idea what that meant.

If there is any one thing I dislike about Twitter then it's the unfortunate similarity it bears to a school playground with its cliques and cool girls, bullies and snobs, in crowd and out crowd. Out there in the virtual world there exists a class system every bit as restricting as the one that still exists in the British social hierarchy, although no one has yet raised an eyebrow and asked, 'Where did you go to school?' This makes it less democratic than it at first appears but there's still plenty of room for everyone and its best far outweighs its worst. It can be a way of seeing behind the scenes at the National Theatre, or understanding the working process an artist goes through, or learning about an event you wouldn't otherwise have heard of, of not feeling lonely when you post a tweet with the hashtag #joinin (a brainchild of comedienne Sarah Millican). It's a new way of going about finding new friends and perhaps meeting them (or not) which sometimes works and sometimes doesn't work quite so well but in my experience at least, it's never a total disaster. Don't rule things like Twitter out on the basis that you think they're purely for the young, or because you know what you like and you know you won't like this. Give it a chance. Like the woman I met at a conference about older women in fashion who told me she didn't know where to find other older women to talk to. 'Get yourself on to social media,' I told her and sure enough, a couple of months later, I got a message back, 'So *that's* where they all are!'

Social media also helps with hunting out that elusive

new job – many agencies and employment websites post positions on a Facebook page or via Twitter and it also makes asking questions easier because they're more accessible. Most larger companies now have social media managers who watch the Twitter feeds like a hawk for bad PR but will equally try to be helpful if you're experiencing difficulties. After one of my periodic rants about age discrimination in the workplace an expert offered to rewrite my CV and I accepted – after all it can't hurt to see what someone else makes of it, and it's entirely possible that the skills I thought were relevant actually weren't. In due course my new, streamlined CV arrived back in my inbox and I sent it off with renewed hope. That it didn't make a scrap of difference to the level of interest in this highly qualified PA was disappointing but nonetheless I'd given it a go so if I was asked again I could truthfully answer, 'Yes, I have tried that'. With the ageism cards stacked so heavily against us I feel it's more important than ever to leave no stone unturned.

The current miracle cure being offered to out-of-work middle agers is *retraining*. The word is sufficiently vague to cover a multitude of different strands but, and pardon my cynicism, this seems to be another of those things that gets launched at us as the answer to all our prayers, like the Age Discrimination Act – and then once it's out there the job is considered done and everyone's happy. At least, that's what I think, although it took me a while to work out what it was about this apparently inoffensive suggestion that put my back up ... apart from the sweeping assumption that if we're out of work then obviously it's because we're no longer good at anything and therefore require re-educating, that is …

However, as a generation we are also branded as reluctant to learn new things (nonsense, I know) and having recommended the 'leave no stone unturned' approach it would be wrong of me to suggest you ignore any help that is offered, whether you agree with it or not. After all, things change at a rate of knots, especially technology; you only need to own a computer and deal with the endless software updates to find that out.

If you're not sure how good your computer skills are then a good way of finding out is to run through one of the online skills tests beloved by employment agencies. They're excellent for pinpointing any weaknesses and cover the full range of office things like Excel, Office, PowerPoint, spelling and grammar. There was a blissful few years where I wasn't asked to do these mini-exams or have my shorthand or typing tested because there was some justification in assuming that I wouldn't be working at the level I was working at if I wasn't competent. Despite stepping off at the top of the PA ladder, those days seem to be gone and I feel sad about that because the respect that came with that about what you had achieved has gone with it. Speaking for myself, I'm also aware that I can be a bit defensive if I'm asked to prove what I can do, or what I've said I can do in my CV, but I suppose it's understandable so if I find myself feeling a bit antsy at an interview the best thing I can do is to ignore it, be nice and remember that the person I'm speaking to doesn't know me and is (hopefully) trying to help.

There is one thing I'm not going to rise above though and that's to do with another middle-age generalisation – the one that says we don't keep up with trends in fashion and spend our days in shapeless things the colour of mud and fog. First up, 'mud and fog' can be very elegant if accessorised correctly and remain a stalwart in my own wardrobe; and secondly, what do you know about how I dress when you've never met me? When I asked an employment agency why they thought so many older women have trouble interviewing successfully, I was told that the way we look and dress plays a part and a far bigger part than we might imagine. That's assuming you get as far as actually speaking face to face with someone, of course. It's surprising and disappointing to be told this, although I suppose not really when you think about how much is decided and assumed within the first few seconds of clapping eyes on someone. We are visual creatures and very often we don't think further than that and I do it as much as anyone, hence my difficulty in meeting the eye of any woman dressed in something bedizened with kittens and paw prints. I assume the agency is basing its opinion on what comes through its own office doors but whatever the reason, the way we look (middle-aged?) is apparently an obstacle to a successful job hunt. How on earth do we get around that? Surely this can't be the case for every type of employment? To stop me exploding an artery I think I'd prefer to view 'the way we look and dress' as more of a reflection on the way we *present* ourselves, which is a fine distinction but one worth making.

The faint whiff of mothballs from a ten-year-old suit isn't going to score us any interview points, I understand that, but we're honestly not helped in this by the far-from-democratic fashion industry. Not that we should feel the need to be cutting edge, if we ever were. What I've found is that as I age I develop a more individual and confident sense of my own personal style. Personal style is a different thing to fashion – although to an extent it does run in tandem with it. If fashion is the horse pulling the style cart when we're younger, then style is the horse pulling the fashion cart when we're older. As we live our lives, growing older and more characterful (and despite the irritating lumping of us into generalised groups) our own style develops to reflect who we are, but the root of it lies in the various fashions we've enjoyed throughout our lives. I think this is wonderful. We ought to know by now what suits us – a rare occasion when you're allowed to say 'I know what I like'.

If, however, we want to shop for actual fashion then that, in truth, has become horribly difficult. Even if we happen to be the right size (6 ... 8 ... 10?) the fit is generally wrong because it's designed for a younger person rather than a mature one and again I speak for myself when I say that my lumps and bumps tend to be a bit south of where they were when I was 25, not to mention east and west. This is true of rather a lot of us, and certainly enough for me to say with some confidence that we are in the majority. In any case our wandering silhouette ruins the line of fitted or tailored clothes bought off the peg because the structure is wrong.

Yes, there are specialist collections for our disobliging bodies but why the hell should we and when did you *ever* see anything in such a shop – or catalogue – that you might conceivably want to buy? The only thing left to us is the shapeless stuff we get criticised for, or Menopause Chic, as I like to call it. Which brings me back to my earlier point about glossy magazines and a general lack of good advice (I'm looking at you, *Vogue*) because if, as a standard run-of-the-mill middle-aged woman, I can't find a size 14 dress that looks halfway decent and fits me properly then surely there's something wrong somewhere. I've been everything from a post-divorce size 6 to a post-op size 16 and the ease with which you can find something when you're tiny is in stark contrast to the problems you encounter when you're a healthy average.

One day, to prove my point, I took myself off to do some incognito shopping and I wrote about it in my *Guardian* column. In the whole entire endless bloody eight-hour day there were only two shops – TWO! – who had anything approaching a decent range of clothes in my size and in only one of those did anyone take the trouble to find out what I was looking for and provide me with help and guidance to find what I needed. If I had bought anything that day that is the shop where I would have bought it. One well-known chain I visited has a website where I've seen sizes 14–18 dwindle to 'out of stock' within hours and yet, in the store itself, there wasn't a thing on the rails over a size 12. When I asked the manager where I could find a size 14 I was told they had larger sizes in the stock room but chose not to put them on the rails. They offered to fetch me something but, honestly, I felt as though I'd been fat-shamed enough and left empty-handed. So much for the purchasing power of the 'grey pound' ...

If I sound angry and unhappy that's because I was ... I am. That fruitless, frustrating shopping trip, coupled with my sudden marginalisation in the wider world was, to put it mildly, unwelcome. Ultimately it threatened not just everything I'd worked hard to achieve but my future, which could be a further 20, 30 or 40 years – who knows? In my day-to-day life things were unravelling at a frightening speed. On my way to appear on the BBC's *Woman's Hour* to talk about how hopeless the work situation was for older women, and wanting to raise awareness by tweeting the experience, I found that my phone had been cut off. The further you fall, the less opportunity shows its hand; in fact it turns its back and ignores you, adding to your overwhelming sense of failure. What you end up doing is setting pride aside and all but begging to be noticed, appreciated, employed ...

At that interview I told it how it is; normally a private person, I felt no squeamishness about setting out the spiral of despair, rationed lavatory paper and unpaid bills in clear, unmitigated terms. It was a rare opportunity to tell women that what we're sold – the softly lit evenings relaxing by the fire with a good book and a glass of Sauternes, the popping off to a show and supper afterwards, the endless river cruises, golfing holidays and deciding which car to buy next or planning the garden's summer colours – is not what most of us will get unless we can change things as they stand now. The fairy tale of a mellow and relaxed middle age is simply not true for the majority who are left to struggle and scrimp and worry about what they did wrong because they're not off to St Petersburg at the weekend but counting down the lean years between when they last earned a wage and finally getting a state pension, by which time who knows what state they'll be in?

Returning to our twin themes of keeping yourself financially afloat and mentally occupied, one obvious solution, should you find yourself surplus to local labour market requirements, is to become a self-employed entrepreneur (the 'olderpreneur' I mentioned in an earlier chapter). We are cheered on to do this (it conveniently kills two government birds with one stone – ageism and unemployment) and a great many of us *do* do it, very successfully, but what can you do if you are an older woman with a brilliant idea and a well-written business plan but you can't raise the finance for a start-up? Not being able to raise finance is a huge barrier for older women (whether they're entrepreneurs or not), unless they already have some money behind them. But it is a fairly stark choice when they have to risk future security against a comfortable present. Some might regard that as a terrific incentive to give it your all and plan carefully but it's also a major deterrent if you're weighing up how far you've got to stretch whatever money you have. When you're already struggling through the frozen wastes of over-50s unemployment it's hard to have much faith in a positive outcome even if you are willing to risk everything you have on turning an inspired idea into reality. Although it is worth bearing in mind that research shows companies in the UK started by older people tend to have a 70 per cent chance of surviving the crucial first five years, compared with 28 per cent started by younger people. What the research doesn't tell us is how many of these successful olderpreneurs are women, or at what age. As with so much of the available research data concerning older women, the detail that would be of most use is missing. However, according to a Barclays Bank report in 2001 'women over 50 are one of the fastest growing groups for business start-up'.

For a woman over 50, working for yourself has a distinct appeal and for a number of reasons but I'd hazard a guess that the majority do it for the flexibility it provides. If you find yourself, as I did, caught up in the failing elderly parent predicament or perhaps wanting an opportunity to spend more time with grandchildren while helping out with childcare then self-employment is the obvious way to go. In my case, I'd done it before with a reasonable degree of success so it seemed not unreasonable to expect the same again, especially when you bear in mind that I'd done most of the getting-off-the-ground spadework for my freelance career already. What I needed was something – part-time, temporary or contract – to fill in while I was slogging through the foothills of building my new career towards a sustainable income. I don't expect to make a fortune – I have perfectly sensible expectations of the standard of living freelance writing is likely to provide me with but as long as it pays the bills then that's fine. I don't fancy a river cruise anyway, but I would like to live without fear of a weekly dunning from the bailiffs and to be able to afford more than toast to live on. I think most of us feel like this. I think we call it 'security'.

I believe what we're aiming for is a gradual easing off, into something more suited to whatever lifestyle we aspire to after retirement. We want to avoid a white-knuckle plunge from the 'cliff-edge of retirement', from full-time employment into long days of twiddling our thumbs and wondering if it's time for *Loose Women* yet. We might want part-time work to balance us while we get our own enterprise off the ground, or to allow our obligations (or wishes) to care for family members to be fulfilled, but whatever we choose we surely do not anticipate putting our feet up and indeed are less and less likely to do that anyway. We're happy to roll our sleeves up and do whatever it takes: work funny hours, stack shelves, sweep streets, anything. Flexibility seems to be the magic word and it's a shame employers haven't caught on to this yet.

But at least we're talking about it; or, rather, a lot of people are talking about it separately. That's why we've ended up with so many different reports all looking at the same thing and drawing similar conclusions. Shouldn't everyone with a stake in this be talking together? Won't that be the way we can change things for the better? We've had long enough to think about it and we've gone all round the houses doing anything and everything other than what we're supposed to be doing and sorting it out. In 1930 John Maynard Keynes suggested that by 2030 we might all be working fifteen hours a week so that everyone had some sort of employment. That's an over-simplified concept and I'm as sure as I can be that it wouldn't work now but it's not a bad idea as preparation for retirement, especially when it's predicted that 50 per cent of the UK population will be over 50 by the year 2020. Surely we owe it not just to ourselves but to future generations as well to fix this, or that 50 per cent over 50 will find themselves at even more of a disadvantage than they do now.

Perhaps of greater and more immediate use to us are the growing number of discussion forums, websites and conferences springing up. I'm thinking in particular of The Age of No Retirement, which has drawn together an impressive array of companies, societies, institutions, charities, thinkers and individuals to take a long, cool look at the current situation, its origins and attendant issues, but in a broad holistic sense rather than picking out whichever problem appears to be the most pressing and fixing that. This seems sensible when so many of the difficulties we face are so tied up with a multitude of other connected problems that were you to attempt to put it down as a diagram it would make about as much logical sense as an Escher drawing. The issues and ideas springing from the first of a series of planned events, which was held in London last year, have now been published and they throw up some interesting thoughts and proposals under eight key areas: Work and Employment; Technology and Communications; Health and Well-Being; The Over-50 Consumer; The Revolution in Long-Term Care; Ageism and Prejudice; Self, Family and Society; and last but definitely not least Knowledge, Education and Learning. It's early days but it's creative and well thought-out and involves many of the stakeholders (that's you and me) who are living with these problems on a daily basis. It seems to me to be very much a step in the right direction.

So, it's not all bad news then. But what can we do in the meantime? Because while it's fantastic that the problems are at last being recognised, none of these reports, debates and discussions help us much in the here and now. When you're facing 50 there is a pressing need to sort out your own personal fiscal policies and a natural inclination to go away and get on with it quietly somewhere, but we mustn't do that – we mustn't take our foot off the gas. If we take ourselves away from the public eye, for whatever reason, we will simply find it more and more difficult to get back there. We need to be visible to reinvent the way we and everyone else thinks about age.

6

A hundred billion neurons

*'Every great and deep difficulty bears in
itself its own solution. It forces us to change
our thinking in order to find it.'*
—NIELS BOHR

Here's a thought: while I'm sitting here noodling about what I plan to write next, how I'm going to frame it and where it fits with everything else I've already written, my brain has been romping through about 1.5 calories every 60 seconds. My brain (and yours) needs about 20 per cent of a resting body's daily calorie intake just to cope with the easy stuff – and that's before you tackle anything even half as complicated as an income tax return.

My doctor told me that when I was sitting in his surgery for a routine check. Only then he did that thing doctors do: 'So how are you otherwise?' he asked and looked at me carefully, which was all the encouragement I needed to release two fat slow tears.

My doctor's smashing. He helped me through my cancer scare and the breakdown that followed surgery, the 'all clear' (unexpectedly emotional) and my recovery – he always makes time for patients who need it. In today's time-pressured world that is unusual, although I wish it wasn't. I also wish more doctors could be more helpful to middle-aged women who are plagued with all sorts of menopausal/physical/psychological problems they don't fully understand, who are largely ignored and left to get on with it. Despite our world being awash with statistics, data streams and listicles, there is so little reliable information about *us* that sometimes we don't know which way to turn.

It is very unusual for me to go bursting into tears in front of anyone – I'm more your private weeper – but when you're on your own and showing the stiffest of stiff upper lips to the outside world it can sometimes come as a bit of a shock when someone asks you how you are. Not in passing at your desk but how you are *really* and it only takes one person being kind to utterly undo you. I know you know what I mean because we all do it. My doctor sat there and listened while I coughed out all my worry and sadness, blew my nose a lot and at the end of it felt moistly better. Then he did what GPs are supposed to do and talked about ways I could perhaps balance things out a bit, distribute the strain of what was an undeniably difficult time a bit more evenly. In passing I'd mentioned how completely knackered I felt when all I was doing was sitting and writing all day and that's when he told me a bit about brains and the energy they need to work, which in turn explained my word count to snacking ratio. Obviously I needed the calories.

All this was news to me. I hadn't thought about my brain needing anything much because I hadn't thought about my brain, full stop. Now I was beginning to think of my brain as something independent, a separate entity from the essence of Me (which was where?) – only I was using my brain to think that. This sort of psychological mind-fuckery can drive you round the bend.

Your brain is clever, whether you think *you* are or not, and yes, in a way it is independent in that it gets on with all kinds of things by itself without you having to waste any time thinking about them. We have between 35 and 48 thoughts per minute, which makes between 50,000 and 70,000 a day, and a lot of them you're not even aware of. No wonder brain scanners showed heads lighting up like Christmas trees when neuroscientists first started mapping our thoughts.

New things about our brains are being discovered all the time and a lot of things we thought were true have been, if not debunked then at least reworked a bit, like that idea announced some years ago that we start losing brain cells from the age of 25 onwards. The good news is that this turns out to be not strictly correct either. The bad news is that we no longer have an excuse for some our dafter moments ...

In recent months I have inexplicably put my car keys in my sock drawer and a pair of socks in my coat pocket (locking myself out of my house at the same time); looked directly at someone I know very well and been completely unable to recall their name; forgotten how to reprogramme the central heating boiler *again*; mislaid a book I needed and been 100 per cent certain it had a green and white spine but which some days later turned out to be red and black, when I located it in the bookcase where it was supposed to be but where I'd forgotten I'd put it. Then there's standing in a room, looking vaguely around and having not the least idea what I went in there for, or starting a sentence without remembering how I meant to finish it, or indeed what I meant to say in the first place. Thankfully, as an habitual self-interlocutor (I'm *thinking aloud*), this mostly happens when I'm trying to reason something out in my head and it's mostly because my grasshopper brain's already moved on to the next thing I wanted to think about. All these things, though, are to do with short-term memory and we notice it more because in middle age we are for the most part far more 'thinky' than we were when we were younger, when our impulses tell us we should actually be *doing* things rather than *thinking* about doing them.

When I started to think about this I had to agree that, yes, I really do spend a lot more time thinking about things than I used to and it therefore follows that because I've got so much going on in my head the impression a passing thought makes could be slight enough for it to slip off and away when my brain makes a sharp turn towards something more interesting. That explains the car keys and the forgetting what I was going to say and it's reassuring to see other people who are not yet middle-aged admitting they've lost the thread or forgotten the question. I have subsequently decided that I'd rather confess than try to muddle through. It avoids me looking like a complete idiot, just a partial one.

It's a similar thing with that business of forgetting what you opened the fridge for, or forgetting why you went upstairs. The current theory is that crossing a boundary by going from one room to another (or opening a door) is what dislodges the original intention and retracing your steps will help you remember. Retracing your steps also has the additional bonus of providing you with some additional exercise, particularly if there are stairs involved.

I've since found that if I make a conscious effort to remember something and embed it properly – like we used to learn things at school, essentially – I generally succeed in dredging it up again correctly some time later. Although panic can scupper that one – there's nothing like the pressure of being put on the spot in front of witnesses to empty my head of everything but tumbleweed.

Lately I've started employing a method recommended by a very dear (and now departed) elderly friend with whom I spent many happy afternoons discussing life and art and getting royally soused. If, for example, he wanted to remember the name of the Mr Hudson who'd just become his heart specialist, he told me he'd think of the Hudson River (he was a New Yorker by birth). To remember that Helen liked two pickles with her vodka – this is the way they drank it in post-war Paris, apparently – then he'd think of my name with two e's and that would remind him. Honestly, the afternoons we spent drinking vodka and eating pickles! I wish I could remember what we talked about …

More confusing, I find, is the yawning gap where I'm perfectly sure I had my relevant fact filed. I know it's there, I think, as my mental fingers probe empty space. This leaves me open-mouthed and gasping like a landed fish because when I began to answer the question I did so in the full and certain knowledge that the necessary info was right there at my fingertips; only now it … isn't. I wouldn't have started speaking if I'd known that was going to happen. Conversely I can haul up something obscure for a question on *University Challenge* with not the faintest idea of where it came from.

Example 1: 'What did you say that tree was called?' Then, after several minutes' failure to identify a common species, 'Erm … give me a minute. It'll come to me. I know this.'

Example 2: On my television screen Jeremy Paxman snaps out, 'Who built the Great Pyramid at Giza?' And a split-second later I yell, 'Khufu.' Boom!

I don't understand. But thank goodness I can remember the weird stuff because the fact that I can is a light in the darkness.

Offering up this evidence I admit that it's tempting to believe what you were told and your defunct and ageing brain cells simply *must* be pouring out of your ears like Niagara but honestly, they're not. The rather wonderful thing about brain imaging is that it shows us something quite different – that our brain sits there between our ears busily occupying itself with reorganising and adapting to our changing requirements as we grow older, gain experience and learn more. It restructures and rewires itself accordingly. It's true that some parts of our brain *do* shrink and lose volume but there is generally a reason for it. For example, our grey matter (the crinkly part where all the cells and whatnot live) carries on streamlining all through our adult years, mainly because of continuing variations in the way each of us uses it to perform the different tasks that help us live our lives. But rather than randomly chucking stuff out, this happens in a carefully structured and organised way. Pertinent to my own career as a PA is evidence suggesting that a middle-aged typist is able to remember bigger chunks of text than her younger colleague, which makes me hopeful that perhaps my own brain is fine-tuning to compensate for my older fingers being a little reluctant to hammer out emails at quite the speed they used to. I like the idea that my brain is looking out for me, spring-cleaning the attic where it keeps all the junk, dusting off the cobwebs and oiling the gears. Although I'm not sure I like the thought of the cells that used to help me when I was younger getting binned because as I grow older I have less use for them. But then in life, if not in my head, I'm a terrible hoarder.

When we were younger, less experienced humans, we needed to be able to make quick decisions based on what we saw, heard and felt in front of us and *not* – and this is the important part – based on our experience and what we'd learned. We older people think just as well as our younger selves but we do it *differently*, using different circuits and different parts of our brains. In fact we think better and more thoroughly than our younger selves. If our decisions are made fractionally more slowly then that's because we have so much more reference material to sift through before we can make a proper risk assessment.

Thinking on your feet is much overrated and unless there's a large predator bounding towards you it's not all that useful. Although let's imagine for a moment that there *is* a large predator sashaying across the plains in your direction: a wise older head will assess size, height and speed, the way it roars, the length of its teeth and claws and then identify this particular beastie as the one with appalling eyesight (like the T-Rex in the film *Jurassic Park*) so standing still is by far the best way to survive, the same way you did when you were in a similar situation five years ago. Your younger self would probably only look at the sharp pointy bits, leg it in panic and finish up as lunch anyway. It's the same way I now know that stoning peaches by pulling a sharp knife inward and towards me will probably end up painful and messy with stitches. And should I come over all absent-minded and forget, I have a sickle-shaped scar on the palm of my left hand to remind me. The day I look at that scar and can't remember how it got there is the day I will start to worry.

David Bainbridge, in his book *Middle Age: A Natural History*, describes the middle-aged brain as 'the most powerful, flexible thinking machine in the known universe'. And it remains as such until we're well into our 60s – which I think is good grounds for a celebratory bout of sudoku.

What I'm doing here, of course, is giving you a massively simplified rundown of what our brains are up to. Advances in science and medicine mean that our knowledge of this most important of all our important organs is expanding much faster than it has before, probably ever (even though there is archaeological evidence that our Neolithic ancestors understood and used trepanning, which doesn't bear thinking about because I can't help wondering what they used for an anaesthetic). Still, despite all our clever science, and however much we do know, there is far more that we don't. Unsurprisingly, to me anyway, a lot of what we don't know has to do with those tricky little beggars, hormones.

To understand more about the labyrinthine and complicated mechanisms that govern the release and regulation of hormones we need to know a little about the other major component in our brain: white matter. White matter sits beneath the crumpled, cell-filled outer layer, peaks in volume during our middle age and doesn't start to decline until we enter our seventh decade, which coincidentally means our middle-aged brain actually *grows* rather than shrinks. White matter is bit like a vast, indecipherable wifi network and is the information highway from one part of your brain to another, which could be right next door or on the other side of your head. That it does this far more efficiently than any wifi network I've ever encountered makes me feel incredibly grateful (and more tolerant of the occasional outage). In the same way that any one person's computer is of limited use without a connection to the Internet, so a single brain cell is only as good as the connections it has to all your other brain cells.

Different bits of your brain do different things. The prefrontal cortex, for example, deals with processes like planning, working out whether the *Rime of the Ancient Mariner* is allegorical and other complex intellectual tasks;

the amygdala sorts out your emotions; the hypothalamus is in charge of hormone production and, dangling off the bottom nearby, is the pea-sized pituitary gland – sometimes called the 'master gland'. There is an intricate, mysterious conversation that goes on between these and other glands in your endocrine system about what to release, how much and when. For instance, triggering the release of the stress hormone, cortisol. This is the hormone previously responsible for prompting you to run away from large carnivorous animals but which is now more likely to flood your system when provoked by tight deadlines and overdue bills. Cortisol is your 'fight or flight' mechanism.

The hypothalamus and its sidekicks are not especially helpful to women in their middle years because they too, of course, are middle-aged and like us they are beginning to think about how they might make life a little less taxing. It helps that we all have a kind of internal clock deciding things like this for us, so puberty, the menopause and other developmental milestones happen in a tightly regulated, limited timespan. Hormones carry the can for an awful lot of what inconveniences us but while it's true that they are the physical drivers behind things like hot flushes, itchy skin, insomnia, weird periods, tearful outbursts and all the rest of it they are merely acting as the brain's foot soldiers. The brain is the boss and it's the brain that fires the menopausal starting pistol, prompted by a reminder from the body clock.

I like to think of the menopause as *middlescence*, as opposed to adolescence, with hormones rushing out instead of in and many of the same feelings and emotions. There is a great deal of similarity between a fifteen-year-old girl and a 55-year-old woman. Also in common with adolescence, we don't have a fat lot of control over how we feel from one day to the next and we kind of just have to roll with it. Different things we do to ourselves in the course of a lifetime might affect how and when we feel what we feel (for instance, did you know that smoking can bring forward the menopause?), and what we eat and drink can help or hinder us quite a bit too, but by and large all these seismic changes are going on quietly in the background, orchestrated by the brain while we're busy with our daily lives. Consequently we only really start thinking about the menopause, possibly the biggest thing that changes for us in middle age, when we actually realise it's happening, when life as we know it begins to slip sideways.

*'It was such a relief to have "not giving
a shit" medically sanctioned.'*
—JENNY LANDRETH, 'OUT THE OTHER SIDE:
ON BECOMING POST-MENOPAUSAL'

The reason I'm talking about the menopause in a chapter about what's going on in our heads is because a lot of the menopause *does* go on in our heads. The shutting down of our reproductive system and the resulting hormonal chaos plays Hamlet with how we think and feel – not least because it reminds us that time is passing. The menopause is no more a purely physical event than puberty is. I wish we talked about it more ... or ever. After all, forewarned is forearmed and whether our experience is good or bad, we'd be better prepared for it. But alas, on the scale of female middle-aged *omertà* the menopause is right up there, at the top, with all the sex stuff. We don't even have fun with it. Where are all our menopause jokes? I feel very let down.

I've read a lot of dry (interesting how often that word crops up in anything relating to middle-aged women) factual stuff about naturally occurring menopause(s) and most of it reads like a 'keep calm and carry on' pamphlet. Lately I've seen quite a bit about the perimenopause, which although obviously as old as the menopause itself seems to be lauded as a new discovery; certainly it's news to me, and I suspect to many others, which just goes to show how woefully neglectful our sources have been.

If, rather than reading about it, you seek personal reassurance that whatever you're going through is all entirely normal, then your chosen human will likely pull a 'eeuw' face and smartly change the subject. Unless they're a medical person, in which case be prepared for an expression of polite boredom to settle over their face. Either way, you'll quickly find out that there is a peculiar etiquette to the business of menopausal fact-finding: apparently it's slightly less bad to talk about it if it's been accomplished via the medium of surgery – that's 'hysterectomy' to you and me – because to undergo an operation means you can officially claim to have been ill and 'battled' through something. But don't go into too much detail and whatever you do, don't go on.

There is hope because it does appear that the menopause 'rules' are slowly being rewritten although it seems we've a way to go when at the click of a mouse I can turn up 7,321 pithy quotes about death (which all of us will face) but only 24 about menopause (which near enough half of us will face). I thought I was done with walls of silence about bodily functions but it seems not. I don't want my daughters and granddaughters to have to grapple with this in the future either. Just tell us what we need to know.

When I look at how things have changed since I was a child I feel hopeful that we will get there eventually but I think we have still to euthanise some behavioural relics from past generations when older women kept schtum about any biological unpleasantness – actual or perceived. The idea of noble suffering has been handed down through the generations and it's something we need to overcome.

When I was finding out about my body, my mum, like so many of her contemporaries, was unable to talk to me about it. She just couldn't say the words, mouthing them in much the same way as Les Dawson did as half of 'Cissie and Ada'. I remember once, when she'd been felled by what I now know was the menopause, being sent off to buy something for her, I wasn't quite sure what, from the chemist. The only thing I knew for certain was that it began with 'san'. I came back with Sanatogen Tonic

Wine because, well, she seemed a bit under the weather, frankly. Of course, what she meant was sanitary towels but she had a complete mental block about saying the words, or even writing them down on a shopping list. I remember feeling mortal embarrassment when, with elaborate semaphore and mime, my mistake was explained to me, and then blushing hotly when I had to go back to the chemist, explain what had happened and come back with a bumper pack of Dr White's. I was, I think, eleven or twelve years old and utterly clueless by today's standards. When I became a mother myself that remembered experience made explaining things properly and openly to my own daughters imperative. It was vitally important to me that they should never be denied the information they needed to understand their own bodies. I did not want them to go through what I went through – what women *still* go through.

But of all the things we need to talk about, the surgical menopause is top of my list. It totally messes with your brain. And the grief: no one tells you about the grief.

The problem with it is an abrupt termination of the pleasant conversation your brain was having with your ovaries about retirement and so on. Things were ticking along gently and amicably and then suddenly ... the ovaries hang up mid-sentence. (In my case, we parted company in St Thomas's over the space of a couple of hours on a Friday afternoon.) There's a brief stunned pause and then all hell breaks loose. I watched Patsy Kensit being interviewed on television just a couple of months after she'd also undergone an emergency hysterectomy. She appeared deeply uncomfortable. She fidgeted and could barely speak. Her words came out rushed and jumbled or hesitant and slurred but such is the ignorance about the aftermath of this procedure that some sections of the media immediately began suggesting that perhaps she was drunk, or worse. I cried. I recognised those feelings. I'd been in exactly the same state not many years beforehand, struggling and bewildered by what was happening to me. Watching another woman flailing around for something safe to hang on to while pandemonium rages internally set a match to all the anger I'd been stacking up ever since it happened to me. I raged and shouted, sobbed and stormed. *It's only what happens when your brain suddenly finds itself, unprepared, in the midst of a catastrophic hormonal shutdown.* 'Only' …? It feels like the End of Days. It's astonishing that teeny tiny things like hormones can scramble the brain so comprehensively and it's equally astonishing that so many of us are wheeled through the theatre doors without sufficient information to anticipate and cope with it. In truth, all you can do is batten down the hatches and wait for the storm to pass, which it will. So will someone please tell us that, because if you try to carry on a normal life in those first weeks afterwards, however strong you think you are, you will fail.

In the UK in a twelve-month period from 2011 to 2012 there were 56,976 hysterectomies carried out in NHS hospitals. That figure does not include procedures carried out in private hospitals, although it does include private procedures carried out in NHS hospitals. (There is no organised system for recording numbers in the private sector.) Of that total number 35,396 are recorded as abdominal hysterectomies and 18,154 as having been carried out vaginally – but no such breakdown is available for the 3,246 hysterectomies carried out in Scotland. The average age for this surgery is 52. Roughly one in five women will have had a surgical hysterectomy by the age of 60, with about 20 per cent of those also having their ovaries removed.

The Hysterectomy Association is currently carrying out three pieces of research on its website, one of which is a Post-Hysterectomy Recovery Survey because 'there is little research information about the impact that having a hysterectomy can have on women'. On a webpage headed 'The Information Needs of Hysterectomy Patients' another survey starts with 'the most common complaint we hear from women who are having a hysterectomy is that they have never been given enough information'. No shit.

The recommended recovery time is six to eight weeks. That's for *physical* recovery – no allowance is made for the additional brain scrambling, the emotional wreckage and the overwhelming grief. I knew about the procedure, the incision, the type of anaesthetic ... but I wasn't told I would wake up in a body that didn't feel like my own. Tubes, drains, catheters, oxygen, drips – all of them feeding things in or taking things out – and a great void somewhere. In hospital I withdrew mentally, cautiously probing my body, feeling for what I knew was missing. It felt as though *everything* was missing. The place at my centre, the safe place where I'd grown my babies, was gone – invaded then taken away and junked.

I'd complained about it often enough when it was there and grumbled about arranging my life around its ebbs and flows – I was baffled that I should feel the loss of my womb so keenly. It sounds mad, and it's quite possible I was, a bit, at the time. The slow burst of saturating grief, the feeling of mourning what now seemed to have been an essential part of *me* became an insistent catch at the back of my mind where it niggled and gnawed and occasionally sluiced me away to a very awful and desolate place. I felt as though I'd been unmothered, unsexed, ungendered ... I felt as though I was in a hundred, no, a *thousand* pieces and I'd have to rebuild myself all over again, which was essentially what I did. Of course not having what I came to think of as my Baby Nest (you see? Mad ...) ultimately, *obviously*, makes no difference at all to who I am as a mother, daughter, sister, friend, a woman ... Perhaps it was an unconscious sorrow for all those unborns who now never would be (not that they would have been anyway) that had me prostrate for days on end. All this I had to work out for myself over a long and lonely stretch of time but if I'd been warned that this may happen, that I might feel like this, that would have helped me to prepare and perhaps I would have come through it with less pain and more understanding.

Just writing these paragraphs makes me want to smash things.

I would have thought that having little choice in the matter – it was the most sensible course of action to remove cancer cells and a large ovarian tumour – would have helped me to come to terms with it, and at the time I did feel as though I would have operated on myself so desperate was I to cut out the disease that had killed my mother. But it's much more complicated than that. I was altogether far too trusting of authority. I thought I could deal with it all on my own so when I asked my consultant surgeon about the impact of my surgery on the menopause and she said, 'your hysterectomy *is* your menopause. It'll save you a lot of bother' I took her at her word. That my consultant was a woman made that statement a double betrayal. Worse, that was twelve years ago and according to the Hysterectomy Association we're *still* not getting enough information? Of course I believed what my doctor told me and I carried on believing it when I was prescribed 'one size fits all' HRT but the thing is, whatever you ingest into your body it will not and cannot replace what the body naturally produces. I thought – because my doctor had said so – that I would escape hot flushes, night sweats, disturbed sleep, weight gain, depression, mood swings, anxiety, brain fag and all the other menopausal delights, but of course I didn't and it's still ticking on now. My body mended within weeks; my brain only caught up a few painful and confusing months later.

There are a couple of other hormones worth paying attention to within this complex, interwoven midlife arrangement – one is slightly helpful, the other not so much. That oxytocin – the nurturing hormone – lowers its rate of production is of benefit because it releases us to concentrate more on ourselves at a time when that's what we really need to do: this is the 'not giving a shit' in the quote at the start of this section on page 169. However, our production of cortisol – the stress hormone – will also reduce, and it will reduce still further should we be suffering from another common menopausal complaint, depression. A lot of women reportedly say they coast through the menopause with nary a backward glance but I've yet to meet one – I've also yet to meet a woman who hasn't suffered from at least some degree of depression during the whole process.

It's tempting to align this whole business with the way older women feel they fit, or not, within society as they age, to look at it as a by-blow of the importance placed on female physical beauty, as we currently define it. To put it very simply and generally, with age men become wealthier, more powerful, dignified and wiser while women growing older sense all that slipping away as their faces and bodies age and they feel themselves becoming more and more irrelevant, apparently. It might not sound like much but the small stuff, such as not being taken seriously (as a consumer, as an employee …), grinds us down and the further down we go the less cortisol we produce to deal with the stress of being on the lower rungs of the social pecking order. It is indeed a vicious circle. Our individual self-esteem, confidence and that word I hate because it sounds so damn earnest – well-being – all matter a great deal and influence our brain's ability to produce what our body needs to function happily and normally. When the body is happy the brain is happy and so, obviously, are we.

Could this be the reason we suddenly start yearning for a change, for roses around the door and a peaceful country idyll – just to escape from the never-ending erosion of who we are? Is it perhaps part of a grand evolutionary plan to take us away from the exhausting business of child-bearing in order to help raise future generations, to pass on our knowledge and experience? Certainly with a decline in the nurturing hormone leaving us with less inclination to let our heart rule our head we're perhaps better placed to deliver some of life's lessons to grandchildren without overburdening them with sentimentality. A falling away of the stress hormone leaves us calmer and less inclined to fight ... maybe, but more of that later.

Personally, I like to think that an (eventually) more serene life post-menopause is the reward we will be given for going through all that other stuff in the first place – not a rational thought perhaps but a nice one. There aren't many other mammals given the benediction of a stretch of relatively peaceful, hopefully less strenuous post-menopausal life – whales (killer and pilot) are among those that do, which makes me very happy because if I'm going to be compared to anything in middle age I'd rather it was a thing of swift and pitiless strength, like an orca, than, say, something old, ponderous, battered and leathery like a Galapagos giant tortoise. I am not ready for my tortoise years. They will come later.

'You must do the things you think you cannot do.'
—ELEANOR ROOSEVELT

Train journeys, although less physically pleasurable than they used to be (sitting down for a long time is not good for my hips), have always provided good opportunities to think, and to indulge in some discreet people-watching – and I do love people-watching. One day, travelling back to London, I had the great pleasure of sitting behind a group of middle-aged women engaged in a lively discussion about … well, you guess. Could it be knitting? The Women's Institute? Lunch and shopping in the Smoke? Perhaps they were talking about *EastEnders* or daytime telly? In fact they were discussing their iPads and related time-saving hacks. They each had an iPad out on the table ('Have you installed IOS8 yet, Janet?'). If we're thinking about overturning clichéd ideas about older women then that seems as good a place to start as any.

Apparently a great many of us are just quietly getting on with things, and it's good that we are but we really ought to be flashing that up on a big screen somewhere … everywhere, in fact. A number of things stop us getting the most out of our middle age and perhaps chief among them is that we allow so many outdated beliefs – that we're opinionated, unwilling to change, slow to learn, irritable, lacking energy and ambition – to continue unchallenged. One of the biggest consequences of that is the trouble we now have finding employment. And employment is one of the things, one of the *main* things, that keep us mentally sharp and in good spirits.

In earlier chapters I've written about the practical and financial consequences of finding yourself out of work in your fifties; and in reality there is no such thing as 'genteel poverty' – a phrase often applied to the middle-aged spinster or widow fallen on hard times. The psychological effects of unemployment can be just as devastating. There is something uniquely awful about you, a busy, industrious intelligent woman, being overlooked for even the most menial positions when you have so much still to offer – regardless of whether you want to hitch your considerable intellect and talent to an employer or utilise it in furthering your own personal ambitions. What makes it so damaging is that this is also a time in life when you have to come to terms with whether or not you've achieved as much as you hoped you would, whether you fulfilled your early promise or not. Not all of success or failure is down to you personally, nor is it necessarily about what you've managed to accumulate materially – that there are different ways of evaluating those two conditions is another thing you begin to view differently as you acquire the wisdom and contemplative brainpower of the middle-aged.

I daresay looking back we all made decisions we regret. Personally, I wish I'd fought harder and longer to retrieve something of more practical use than a set of silver teaspoons and my mother's tablecloth from my fifteen-year marriage. If I'd been more ruthless then maybe I could have kept a toehold on the property ladder, instead of watching that ladder grow longer and longer until the prospect of home ownership disappeared away into the clouds, possibly forever. But the art of ruthlessness was something I had yet to learn when I was 35 and now, understandably, one of the things most occupying my 59-year-old brain is how on earth I will ever keep a roof over my head and remain independent in a place I want to remain independent in for as long as I possibly can.

I couldn't envisage even the beginnings of a plan of escape from London. As my hopes for another job withered on the ageism vine, I decided that what I had to do was move out of London and back to the countryside where I was convinced I would be happy, where I could work in peace and quiet, with my family nearby and a cheaper cost of living – but, ironically, where there was almost no chance at all of ever finding a part-time job: I would have to commit myself 100 per cent to building a career as a writer. But every time I tried to think my way around it I came up against the same set of difficulties, and most insurmountable of these was that I was boracic, skint, broke, virtually destitute. My brain followed its well-trodden path back to securing a temp assignment, or short contract, by which I could earn the means to engineer my release. My brain needed to climb out of its rut.

One thing the older head is particularly good at is thinking differently – being inventive, creative and exploring unfamiliar intellectual landscapes. The body might be slowing down a bit, working a 55-hour week might no longer be possible (or desirable) but your brain is frolicking around new ideas like a winter-fed cow turned out on to new spring grass. This is an enormous benefit and, for me, one that continues to surprise and delight. I've gone from being one of those children for whom the regular aptitude tests inflicted on us in the '60s represented a recurring nightmare to being an adult who can think laterally. It's brilliant – nothing short of miraculous and a constant source of wonder to me. I have to keep reminding myself that I *can* solve the *Only Connect* wall, that I *can* do the MENSA test, that by taking a little time when I'm reading something complicated I can grasp an abstract theory and understand it. Mental arithmetic and chemical formulae continue to elude me but, hey, you can't have everything and my brain seems not to have much 'numbers' wiring, although the delightful thing is that I know enough about other stuff to allow me to arrive at the answers by an alternative route. I can concentrate and focus and forget all about eating and other mundanities. Although, and this is important, if I spend too much time on Twitter before I begin any freelance work I will find my attention span shortened accordingly and I will probably also find my productivity falls as a result. Twitter is not *the* answer, although it will often provide *an* answer. It just won't be an original thought crafted by you.

Being in work doesn't only benefit mental acuity – our modern age of fractured social and familial networks, of marginalisation and loneliness, means going out to do a job also provides some welcome social interaction with other people. You might not crave 'interaction' per se – and a lot of people, old and young, don't – but the value of mixing with different groups brings gains outside of what you might want for yourself and it's worth remembering that. Working at home is heaven but I find that after a solid week of it I start to feel a bit alien in the outside world and it takes me a while to adjust to being in 'unfamiliar' surroundings and actually talking to people. I play blind man's buff around my social skills, clumsily identifying each one and then whipping off the blindfold to become a fully formed human being again.

Certainly I find another oft-reported middle age brain symptom to be absolutely true: it really does take me a bit longer to adjust. My personal body clock is a good case in point. After a decade in roles where my working days were very different from the normal nine to five – rocking up at the office late morning and often not signing off until past midnight – it's taken me several months to adjust back to a more usual daily rhythm. I suppose I could reasonably argue that that *was* my natural diurnal rhythm were it not for the fact that recently I've felt it necessary to go to bed and get up at more recognisably normal times because I've begun nodding off on the sofa by 10.30pm. I enjoyed my stay-out-late lifestyle and it suited me very well for several years but it no longer fits with how my brain is telling me I should live my life now. Although I suppose that could simply be my age.

Intriguingly, without the rigours of high-level PA-ship occupying my head there are the things I thought I'd forgotten popping back up again all bright and shiny – like how to read music, play the tenor recorder, perform a dance routine to 'Sisters' (learned as an eight-year-old) and the reams of poetry I've committed to memory over the years. Some of the things I used to be able to do I've had to remind myself of – like speaking French, baking a Dutch apple cake or drawing a horse. But it's all still in there, in my head, where eventually I will find it again once I've dusted and rewired my neural pathways. That's called neuroplasticity and it's another thing I've discovered my brain can do.

Neuroplasticity is when your brain reorganises itself, adapting to things that have happened to it. That might be down to an injury or it might simply be because you've begun thinking in different ways (like when you retire or move to a new environment). If you're right-handed and something happens to stop you using that hand (a broken wrist or a stroke) you will eventually, and with practice, be able to use your left hand just as competently. If you're right-handed and never use your left hand, that's called 'learned non-use': you were able to use both equally well in your early years, you've just learned not to because it's easier and faster. It's a case of 'use it or lose it', with the skill there – just unused and atrophied. When something happens which blocks the routes your brain usually travels down to accomplish things, it simply comes up with its own diversion and drives around it. It takes time and practice from you but if you keep physically signalling what you need to do then your brain will generally work it out. I find that piece of information tremendously reassuring. I'm thrilled to know that my brain won't take no for an answer either.

This news that we *can* train our brains to perform better, that we continue to learn, means we can teach older brains new tricks. Here's the thing, though: I don't like, indeed I have developed a strong aversion to, those very boring handheld plastic brain trainers that used to be advertised all over the place. I still see older people fiddling with them on the train but I don't understand why our years mean we must have something different – in fact recent research shows that older people resent this kind of 'special' treatment and go out of their way to avoid it. I think we can agree that it's much more interesting and challenging to find ways of training your own brain in your own way. That should be vastly more entertaining than somebody else's generic ideas about what our heads should be doing. For instance, apparently hand-eye coordination deteriorates with age but I say bring on the Angry Birds or Tetris to deal with this. Anything that makes you do things that are new, different and stimulating will help – even something as ordinary as changing your daily routine will make you concentrate and use your brain instead of drifting around on autopilot. It's also the case that many people now have a tablet and/or smartphone so the possibilities for putting your brain through an interesting and comprehensive workout wherever you happen to be are more or less limitless. There are memory games, maths games, art games, *game* games, games that involve blowing things up (useful if you're feeling cross), word searches and crosswords – every sort of game you can imagine. You might not get very far with your first few attempts but persevere and you'll be an Angry Birds ninja before you know it. A couple of caveats though: once you've got used to a game and it becomes automatic it means your brain's cracked it and it's no longer doing what you want it to do – so move on to a new one, or a different permutation of the old one. Also, it's perfectly possible to develop an addiction to one or all of these things – they've been designed that way – and overworking a middle-aged hand and arm may result in tennis elbow, frozen shoulder, repetitive strain injury, etc., etc. You might also burn the dinner, which is much more serious.

Speaking of the more physical side of things, that too can have an effect on your brain's liveliness. If you insist on sitting around and becoming a couch potato then your head will be only too happy to oblige. But keeping yourself reasonably fit and active has an extremely positive effect on your brain. In addition to requiring calories to function properly, your brain also requires 20 per cent of any oxygen you take in – obviously the more and better quality the oxygen you take in the friskier your brain will feel. Plus, anything that increases blood circulation is a good thing. I learned a lot from my father and one of the most important things he (unintentionally) taught me is that a daily walk, or the equivalent, keeps you fit and well in more ways than one. As I mentioned previously, he was out early every morning, in any weather, walking a four-mile round trip. He was still hiking up the Derbyshire peaks well into his 80s.

I struggled a bit when dad took up the guitar and then the ukulele but getting his stiff woodsman's fingers to hold down the chords was only part of the exercise as far as he was concerned – remembering them in the first place was his main objective. (It was hard on any listening musical ear though.) In his final years, when he lost his voice, we found it easier to conduct our weekly catch-up via Skype so that I could see his face and better understand him. And yes, he had an iPad and a computer, although he never trusted the Internet sufficiently to do any shopping on it – but then he didn't use ATMs either, for the same reason. I suppose in your ninth decade you can afford to pick your battles.

In terms of what you think you might achieve in middle age (and later) the news that you can rejig your brain, and that your brain rejigs itself, removes so many of the limitations and boundaries we think apply to us. This is particularly true for women of our generation who until now might not have had enough time to themselves to do the things they wanted to do. And even if we are pulled back into caring for grandchildren or our own parents there are still opportunities to tackle new things and expand horizons. I'd say it's an essential part of middle-aged life. Between the various crises of the past couple of years the thing that's helped keep me sane is discovering (and rediscovering) occupations and subjects that are involving, demand concentration and require me to use my brain. I've rekindled a half-decent relationship with art, mostly on the iPad, which allows greater creative freedom and means I don't, for now, have to buy any extra equipment or supplies. I gradually got my head around studying again, absorbing myself in things I would have considered dull a few years ago but which now fascinate me, I think because I now have far greater patience. I'm sure it's no coincidence that there's been such a rise in the number of mature students, either on campus or via distance learning programmes. If I were to draw a comparison with Lester Burnham and his pleasure in surprising himself with rediscovered abilities then I'd say that finding my brain can absorb new concepts and ideas like a new sheet of especially absorbent blotting paper is perhaps the most pleasing.

Aside from injury, stress is perhaps the biggest enemy of a properly functioning brain and stress is also, alas, particularly prevalent in middle-aged women. Middle age, for all the reasons I've outlined in the various parts of this book, can prove extremely stressful for women. Prolonged stress can actually cause brain damage, albeit temporarily, by flooding the brain with cortisol, which distracts and prevents its ongoing repair programme while at the same time increasing a process called 'synaptic pruning' – a sort of tidying-up procedure which is exactly as it sounds. As if that wasn't enough, cortisol is one of the main culprits in causing us to put on weight – that is, assuming you're not scarfing down a big bar of chocolate every other night. Which I suppose you might be if you're feeling particularly stressed, because that's another way this 'fight or flight' hormone makes certain that when the occasion arises we'll be able to do exactly that. Our rising cortisol is telling our brain that we're about to have (or are currently having) a crisis so the brain starts laying in backup energy by way of stacking any spare calories around our middles and encouraging us to find some more – this is what's known as comfort eating. My own middle bears ample evidence that I have recently spent quite a lot of time dealing with one crisis or another and that my brain has been not waving but drowning … in cortisol.

It may be that floundering around in stress hormones is what's helped me to shed those troublesome inhibitions I've spent my life hauling around. I no longer worry about the possibility of looking foolish or embarrassing myself – although that could equally be because I no longer care all that much about what people think of me. In any case, what that means to me is that when I'm faced with something new to learn now I can just get stuck in rather than walking around and around the edge, unable to commit one way or another. It's about thinking (and saying) 'yes, absolutely, I would *love* to do that' and then actually doing it.

Learning anything new works best if you can immerse yourself in it completely, whether it's a new language, a computer game, bridge or the ukulele. If you can do that you will focus your mind on that one thing, hopefully producing the result that what you want to remember will go in and stay in. Remember what I said about making a conscious effort to remember something so that it makes a substantial impression to hold it in your head? It's that. Don't try to do one thing while you're thinking about something else. If you're writing an email then write the email and think about it while you're doing it, that way you're going to avoid placing an inappropriate kiss on the end of your missive to your local council, or typing 'basmati rice' instead of 'best wishes'. I know women can multi-task but sometimes it's best not to.

One thing I luxuriated in when I stepped down from the *Guardian* was having time to think again – 'what is this life if, full of care, we have no time to stand and stare'. Indeed. And I can very easily slip into a meditative state while I'm looking out of the kitchen window and doing the washing up, or if instead of trying to break records with the speed I can get round my own daily walk (thanks, Pa) I can stop, look at things and just allow my mind to spin slowly and freely through random thoughts. It helps my brain to be creative when I want it to be. Call it day-dreaming if you like but it's so much more than that, *and* it helps to bring down stress levels. We all need such moments of mental absence; they keep us level – and so does having a bloody good laugh at something, even if it's with a dark, wry humour at things going catastrophically wrong. There has to be balance while you're performing the high-wire act of middle age. If there isn't, you fall off. Don't worry, though, because you're not going to.

Looking back to where I went wrong, I think it was in allowing it all to get on top of me. Yes, I got a double dose of *annus horribilis* with bells and whistles but I'd also forgotten about quite a few of the things I've written down here. I did find some escape and mental peace in walking and you see so much more of London, or anywhere else for that matter, when you start walking around and looking about you. I was grateful for having Greenwich Park on my doorstep, although I tried to avoid the times when I knew it would be throbbing with tourists. In winter I would go with my coat pockets stuffed with peanuts, for there is much enjoyment to be had in watching a squirrel take a nut out of a shell. Sometimes people would speak but on the whole Londoners tend to wrap themselves deep in their coats and not utter a word – after fifteen years I thought of myself as a Londoner and followed suit. After my father died and we scattered his ashes into the Suffolk river he loved, I would go and stand on the Royal Steps in front of the Old Royal Naval College and look out over the Thames as it bent away, round towards the Thames Barrier and on to the sea and I would feel close to him.

I did a lot of dwelling on things and self-analysing standing there, looking at the river, but while I was doing that I was wasting time. It was time to set things right. Time to move on.

7

Skin

'I'm tired of all this nonsense about beauty
being skin deep. That's deep enough. What
do you want, an adorable pancreas?'
—JEAN KERR

I like my face. Aside from its first few formative years on this earth, it's the same face I've had for 59 years, more or less. Although – and I hope you're sitting down – recently I discovered that in fact the only things about me that are the same me as the me I was 50 years ago are my DNA and, if I still had them, my eggs. How so? You may well ask, and just to annoy you I will reply with a further question: did you know that in the course of a year your body replaces 98 per cent of its atoms? 98 per cent! What this means is that I send a goodly proportion of my constantly renewing skin cells gurgling off down the plughole every time I shower or wash my face, and God alone knows how many I slough off after a good scrub with the loofah. Doesn't that make spending a sizeable chunk of the cash earned with the sweat of my (relatively new) brow on fighting the seven signs of ageing a slightly redundant action? I mean, even my blood cells are never more than a few months old. My bones – my *actual* bones – rebuild themselves over anything between two to seven years. I am so amazed at the very thought of this I think my freshly recalibrated neural pathways might explode.

As we age what actually changes about us is not so much our skin but the way that skin is manufactured and maintained by our amazingly efficient and thoughtful bodies. The problem, if there is one, is not so much what we put *on* but what we put *in* – as in, what we eat. Which probably explains why, even at my advanced age, I can still erupt in pimples if I truffle my way through an entire tub of salted caramel ice cream. My name is Helen, I'm almost 60 and I still get spots.

We know this though, don't we? You are what you eat and all that? So how is it that in the last twelve months we've somehow managed to part with a whopping £2.2 billion for cosmetic skincare in the UK alone? That's skincare, not cosmetic surgery, which continues to guzzle our cash at an equally terrifying rate, growing from a 'mere' £750 million in 2005 to a staggering £2.3 *billion* in 2010 (it's predicted to top £3.6 billion in 2015). Somebody somewhere is doing awfully well off the back of our insecurities, not to mention our gullibility, although this clearly doesn't trouble us a great deal if the profits generated are anything to go by. Women, and especially older women, have been minutely scrutinised under the Microscope of Aesthetic Perfection and found wanting in such diverse areas as eyes, brows, lips, teeth, nose, chin, ears, hair (head), hair (body), neck, breasts, cleavage, back fat, belly button, tummy, buttocks, thighs, knees, hands, bingo wings, elbows, nails, feet, toes and finally, because obviously there's room to squeeze in just one more *teensy* profit margin, our genitals. Yes, you too can have your lady love tunnel surgically tidied into a handsome designer vagina for a reasonable sum, or on credit if you can't quite manage the whole lot in one go. How wonderfully considerate.

In the US the most common reason given for undergoing a facelift is that the patient wants to look younger in a tough, competitive job market. I don't see that we're all that far away from resorting to similar measures on this side of the pond, not when you consider how ruthless our own recruiters are about replacing the steady (slightly wrinkled) hand of experience with the impetuous (but smoother) hand of youth, although it's hard to see how this addresses the problem of getting your application looked at in the first place. (Perhaps in the future we'll be adding photographs to our list of qualifications, something that is frowned upon now.)

On the bright side, at least the UK does not appear in the 2013 top ten nation rankings for the number of cosmetic procedures carried out. Unsurprisingly the US occupies the top slot with Brazil coming a close second – that's Brazil, with its favelas and widespread poverty. In a compelling 2013 documentary for the *Unreported World* strand on Channel 4, it was explained that Brazil now has ten times more plastic surgeons than the UK and procedures have increased by 40 per cent in two years. Even allowing for the disparity in population size (203 million as against 64 million) that's a lot.

In Brazil the two reasons women most commonly give for seeking to have cosmetic surgery are wanting to have a 'bikini body' or a body they feel will improve their chances of getting a job. Over and over again in the course of the programme I heard variations on the theme that if a Brazilian woman doesn't fit the current perception of the perfect body then her prospects for career advancement are pretty much zero, even to the extent of having a nose narrowed if it is considered too wide and too 'black' – a disturbing progression of the US facelift approach to getting a job mentioned above. A wide definition of what constitutes 'reconstructive surgery' helps those trying to leapfrog their way up a health service surgical waiting list – for example, a woman who has had a child can have a 'reconstructive' tummy tuck, while a woman showing signs of 'psychological distress' over her small breasts can have them augmented. If a woman can't afford her surgery she can apply to have it subsidised or carried out free in one of Brazil's public hospitals, or take out a payment plan if she doesn't want to wait. None of the women interviewed for the programme could be considered wealthy but all regarded aesthetic surgery as not just an essential step towards bettering their lives but a very desirable one. In Brazil, cosmetic surgery is regarded as a symbol of status. In Brazil, 'beauty' is everything.

It's worth noting that these things happen in the UK too and that the NHS carried out breast augmentations amounting to a cost of around £52 million in 2013. The number of these procedures has risen by 145 per cent over a decade and although many will be for vital reconstructive surgery following breast cancer, those figures only account for a fraction of the overall number.

The way we see ourselves, our joy and pleasure in a healthy body, our pride in ageing well and our survival are all undermined by a pernicious propaganda plastered throughout advertising and the media. In the course of a day it's said that women look at between 400 and 600 adverts. They're everywhere – you simply can't escape them. What's more we live in a world where any model agent worth their salt knows very well that if they receive a casting call for 40-year-old models they should send women at least ten years younger than that. If you look at any catalogue, any website, purporting to be for the over-50s you will see clothes modelled not by inspiring, characterful, beautiful women of our own age but by bland 30-year-old size 10 models in polyester dresses with 'clever ruching'. Aside from the fact that polyester is to menopausal women (pre- and post-) as garlic is to a vampire, what we see is not representative. What are we supposed to make of it? Do they think that seeing clothes on a stereotypical younger woman will persuade us that in this horrible garment we will magically conform to their gold standard and look the same? Do they think we came down with the last shower? To rub further salt in our wounds, the 'younger model' rule seems not to apply to men – our male counterparts get 'silver foxed' by a 'gentleman's outfitter'. The next catalogue to fall out of my Sunday paper following these rules will be used to line the cat litter tray.

The practice of applying creams and lotions to maintain our dewy youthfulness is, of course, almost as old as the hills. We were making herbal infusions to keep hair bouncy and shiny long before advertisers began suggesting that if we used a particular brand of shampoo washing our hair could be transformed from a boring, messy experience into something akin to having orgasmic sex under a waterfall. Rubbing stuff into our faces began millennia before anyone mentioned collagen or crow's feet and we did it mainly to stop our skin blistering off in unfriendly weather, which seems sensible. The belief that in doing so we can nail fleeting youth to the spot and stave off the predations of age is, in the whole history of the human race, a relatively recent phenomenon.

I'm inclined to believe that painting our faces (and bodies) is an even older practice but in, say, the last 600 years, we've run mad with the idea – going on to poison ourselves with white lead *maquillage*, squirt belladonna (deadly nightshade) into our eyes, scrub our teeth and freckles with lemon juice and salt, shave off our eyebrows and draw them back in again, paint our lips with crushed beetles, go to great lengths to remain pale and untouched by the sun (a sign of wealth and status) and then gone to even greater lengths to get ourselves permanently suntanned all over (a sign of wealth and status). We've stuck mouse-skin spots on our faces to hide pox scars and, as a precursor to our current obsession with dental aesthetics, we've experimented with various forms of false teeth and veneers, among them wooden teeth and teeth extracted from the dead at the Battle of Waterloo. In more recent times, we've had all our teeth extracted as a 21st birthday present and false teeth fitted to 'save trouble later on' (I'm told my grandmother did this). These days we glue things to our teeth and bleach them to dazzling, eye-scorching whiteness, which I suppose is progress of a sort.

Our hair has been fashionable in styles long, short, curly, straight, shaved back from our foreheads, braided, plucked, dyed and sprayed. For years my father greeted news that I was arriving for a visit with 'And what colour's your hair now then?' Understandable when it's been pretty much everything since I could first wield a dye brush, or pay someone else to do it for me.

Body hair hasn't escaped. Even our current fixation with removing each and every follicle from every conceivable surface isn't quite a first: there is evidence to suggest that the presence of pubic hair on the female body was considered 'uncivilised' in ancient Greece, Egypt and Rome (but only if you were upper class). Ancient Middle Eastern and African cultures also routinely removed pubic hair. And then the whole business fizzled out for a bit during the Middle Ages when if it was done at all it was accomplished by plucking and was usually performed for the practical reasons of hygiene and curtailing the activities of lice rather than out of snobbery.

Whether a furless muff is common practice in *our* middle ages I couldn't possibly say but I can tell you that middle-aged pubic hair is one of the reasons for this book. A reader wrote to ask if, as she was considering advancing her new relationship to the next level, it would be necessary for her to book a Brazilian or similar. The correct answer is, of course, no, not unless you want to. But in the course of my enquiries someone told me that all your pubes fall out by the time you're 60 anyway (meaning mine are on borrowed time). I haven't been able to disprove this startling piece of information because while there are entire style guides on various forms of pubic topiary for the modern young woman about town, there is nothing at all of any practical use to anyone who wishes to reassure themselves about the future prospects for their own, more mature lady garden. However, after exhaustive research I can inform you that as with so much else in older life, sometimes it does fall out and sometimes it doesn't, and whether it does or it doesn't is down to hormone levels and genes. I think. Mostly it seems just to lose ... volume – so not so much a bush any more as a patch of blasted heath.

My point is that it's a pretty poor story should you find your nethers disconcertingly chilly one morning with no reassurance readily to hand on our splendid data highway. There's loads of stuff about vajazzling, but not so much about the life expectancy of a natural winter pelt. And while we're on the subject, did you know that, should you wish to, you can freshen your foof with a DIY 'vagacial' for less than a fiver (physically awkward, I'd have thought, for those of us who are less bendy), or, if you really want to hooray your haha, you can have a salon 'Peach Smoothie' for a mere 35 quid? I bet you're thrilled, and not just by my knowledge of appropriate euphemisms. I related this astonishing piece of research to the editor and his deputy at my *Guardian* leaving party, together with the useful information that there exists in London's Covent Garden a man who will fit you with a tailor-made merkin should you be unfortunately lacking in the relevant area and find your self-esteem withering as a result.

Far too often it feels to me as though we're being bullied out of our free will; that barely a day goes by without a further tweak to the law of supply and demand in relation to female beauty and what defines it. Perhaps this is the price we pay for the speed at which we disseminate information: the latest trend, the newest false eyelash, the latest shade of lipstick. There is hardly time to determine an individual look before the whole circus has moved on to the next thing, but don't you think that what we do, or don't do, with our bodies is for us to decide rather than big business? I honestly have no problem with anyone having cosmetic surgery, tattoos, piercings or whatever *for the right reasons*. When I feel my heart breaking is when I see a 40-year-old woman being put through an eye lift because she's convinced that her ever-so-slightly droopy eyelids are the only thing standing between her and a successful, fulfilling relationship – and doing the whole lot from consultation to procedure to recovery in front of cameras for our televisual enjoyment. I've no idea whether she was right about her eyelids but I suspect not and the programme chose not to tell us.

Why do we blame perceived physical defects for holding us back or believe that the way each one of us looks is not 'beautiful'? Beauty is such a subjective thing. It seems we've dictated and narrowed the definition to such an extent that we can't be allowed to deviate from it. How dull would it be if everyone became Stepford Wife identikit perfect? How frightening is a future where we allow the spheres of marketing and film to shape and dictate the standard we should aspire to? Aren't marketing and film supposed to sell us escapism, dreams, fantasies ...?

It might sound far-fetched but you can, if you wish, have any bit of you remodelled as whichever film star or model you like, if you have the money. The current spate of young women surgically altering themselves to look like living Barbie dolls or Manga anime characters is a similar phenomenon. But what happens when anime and Barbie are obsolete as aspirational models for feminine beauty? Will we then become dated by the type of procedure we've had done – last year's lips, old-fashioned noses, out-dated breasts? Will we start paying to have our unfashionable bodies and faces updated season by season, like buying a new winter coat? Moreover, are we saying that you can only be as beautiful as the size of your bank balance? That you can be £5,000 worth of beautiful or £20,000? And what about when age begins to catch up with you, which it will: what will be your worth then? It seemed eccentric and funny in the 1985 film *Brazil* but Terry Gilliam's futuristic vision now feels uncomfortably prescient.

When you look back through history you generally find that some imperfection or other is the precise reason a woman was considered beautiful in the first place. Generally speaking, our faces are not symmetrical and they're not meant to be – try putting your hand over one side of a face in a photograph, then switching sides and you'll see what I mean. I love doing that – in a way it's quite revealing. Having a perfectly symmetrical face might sound as though it should be attractive but it actually looks a bit weird and, really, it's not beautiful. The changing face of beauty, real beauty, is lit up by gap-toothed smiles (Lauren Hutton, Georgia May Jagger, Lara Stone), perfectly placed moles (Cindy Crawford, Eva Mendes, Marilyn Monroe), monobrows, squinting and oddly coloured eyes (Frida Kahlo, Karen Black, Heidi Klum), a too-wide mouth (Sophia Loren – in her own words), high/low/small/voluptuous bosoms, big and little bums or bums that are somewhere in between. I could go on but I'm sure I don't need to.

Evolution fixed it so that like almost every other living creature we spend a good deal of time looking around for our perfect mate, or the closest we can get to it. (Incidentally, it's fascinating to look at how many people look like their partners.) We do it instinctively and in order to perpetuate our genes, but if we start looking for physical perfection all the time I reckon we'll end up as a largely asexual species, which would be very boring. Perfect is not sexy – sexy is something else and often Cupid's arrow arrives in the form of things called pheromones. You can't see pheromones because they're too small but you can buy them in a bottle of perfume and I read somewhere that sex-on-legs actor Steve McQueen actually wore pheromone aftershave. Everything has a price tag ...

Last year I met a refreshingly honest skin doctor at a conference. He'd worked in skincare research and development for most of his professional life and his advice to me (or to anyone else for that matter) was to find the cheapest moisturiser I liked and use that, because whatever a brand claims, moisturising is basically as far as you will get with any of it. All the add-ins like brand, scent, texture and packaging, he said, are window dressing and none of the 'science' amounts to a whole lot of anything very meaningful. And in any case, the skin buffed and glowing on my face now will all be gone in a few weeks' time: I'll have sloughed it off and grown myself a lovely, radiant, fresh new layer – lines and all – with or without the assistance of a 90 quid pot of anti-ageing bee bile, or whatever the new wonder ingredient might be.

I go to a lot of exhibitions and conferences to learn about new ideas and products. It goes with writing about fashion and beauty and women. It's a subject that is genuinely of great interest to me, and it has been ever since I can remember, but I can't help noticing that as I've grown older my feelings about it all have changed. In 2013 I was invited to something called the Anti-Ageing Health & Beauty Show and very fascinating it was too, although perhaps not in the way the organisers intended.

I hadn't been to such a thing in the UK before and I wasn't at all sure what to expect but what I had definitely not expected was that it would give me a peculiar wobble about my age before I'd even got through the doors. Walking from Olympia Underground station as only one in a large group of women – all of us of 'a certain age' and all of us heading in the same direction for the same reason – I was surprised to have this thought: 'I don't belong here. This is not me. I am not this age'. It was an angry, mutinous 'bugger off and leave me alone' thought. But it was also what this industry feeds off – our fear that we're missing something, that we're left behind and somehow redundant.

Inside the hall wasn't nearly as bad as I thought it would be, and it was busy – of course it was. One of the more positive memories I have of the event is recognising that there is something really quite magnificent about a few hundred older women all together, *flocking*. I imagine it's because we don't do it very often but we should because the feeling of camaraderie is delicious and something to enjoy; but this was still early in the day …

There were a lot of stands for nutrition, healthy eating and mineral supplements. There were a lot of stands for exercise, clothing and make-up. There were far too many stands for the hokey stuff – the snake oil – including a bee venom 'natural facelift in a jar' (no bees harmed), snail slime moisturisers (Korean farmed snails), machines to pinch, pull and manipulate your face and computer screens to tell you how old your skin really is. (We've just been through all that – not very old at all.) There were rows of women lying on couches having their teeth whitened. There was a queue around the block for Botox and fillers being offered at a knockdown sale price … Yes, that's right, fillers and Botox being administered in a canvas tent in the middle of an exhibition space with no pre-consultation, no visible certification of the practitioners and no follow-up appointment afterwards to make sure having your face pumped with toxins hasn't affected you in any kind of adverse way – and I daresay you had to sign a form saying you wouldn't sue them if it did.

This middle section of the hall, where the quick surgical fixes and new treatments were on offer, began to feel more and more like the Wild West as the day wore on. The sales pitches became louder and more evangelical and a sense of time-critical desperation began to creep in. By about four o'clock in the afternoon there was near-hysteria. It was like mass brainwashing and it was hard to distance myself from it. It felt panicky and horrible. There were genuinely interesting, useful talks going on around the quieter margins but the noisy centre block was where pushing through the crowds was hardest, where the queues wound endlessly through the aisles and where women – young and old – were congregating under the lights, by all the shiny things. Like so many magpies.

On the way home, when I was out and could clear my head, I worked out why I'd felt so out of sorts on the way in (and on the way out). It was the way I was being dictated to, instructed to do any or all of these expensive, sometimes physically invasive things in order to remain valid as a woman. All the things I had achieved, and had yet to achieve, in my life: motherhood and grandchildren; the pieces of my art tucked away on painted-over bathroom walls; the wedding dresses I'd designed and made; the little scribbles of published writing crisping in my cuttings folder; the films, the dancing and the fun; the suffering and surviving; the sheer unremitting bloody struggle of it all; all of that counted as though for nothing against the tightness of my jawline. It was a profoundly distressing thought.

I've been mostly ignored by the world at large since I hit middle age, left without a job, blanked by the fashion industry, made an irrelevance, and all because I dig my heels in and refuse to be coerced into this ridiculous, hopeless grasping at the way I *used* to look? For looking like the 59-year-old woman I am happy and proud to be? You've got to be kidding. It'll take more than hyped-up promises about rejuvenated skin and perky tits for me to play nice. I'm done with 'nice'.

☙

'The finest clothing made is a person's own skin, but, of course, society demands something more than this.'
—MARK TWAIN

I remember being invisible before now. I was often invisible as a child, especially when I was in trouble for something. I was invisible quite a lot during my late 30s 'hippy nouvelle' phase – mostly floaty frocks and Doc Martens' worn with mad hair so hardly surprising really (ironic when you're dressing to be noticed though). But as a woman who enjoys her own company, invisibility is a skill I've actively cultivated because, let us not forget, invisibility is also a super power.

On those days when I would rather not speak to anyone, to discover I can more or less vaporise in a room full of people is rather thrilling. On the other hand, waiting to be served in a shop while being ruthlessly ignored is not thrilling at all, it is disheartening and depressing and a lot of other d-words as well. It's interesting though, isn't it, how some days you go through life as you always have when on others you seem to fade from view? I've carried out a few experiments over the years to test the boundaries of my apparent gift for vanishing-ness. The answer, mostly, seems to be lipstick.

I'd had my suspicions about this for some time but one day a couple of years ago I set out to prove my theory by spending a day in my preferred retail temple of dreams – Selfridges. In the morning, I progressed around the store clad in my habitual black, fully made up with eyeliner and so on, and wearing a natural lipstick. To anyone who cared to notice me, I was a smartly dressed middle-aged lady who spent a whole morning browsing on different floors entirely, blissfully and completely alone, untouched and untroubled by human interaction of any kind and especially untouched by shop assistants. After lunch I went to buy a new lipstick (I like the expensive sort in a decadent case – it is A Weakness) and I had it professionally applied by the assistant, when I managed to find one. This lipstick was poppy bright and scarlet and shiny – and all afternoon I had doors opened for me, help offered, little chats here and there with fellow shoppers and sales staff, various free samples foisted on me … it was a revelation. So there it is, conclusive proof of both invisibility and the power of a red lipstick. Sort of … But how you dress and present yourself does make a difference to your level of invisibility. If I dress to be invisible then I *am* invisible and I'm not surprised by it. Unfortunately, dressing to be invisible also means dressing and making up like a middle-aged woman, so I proved something else too.

There is a practical problem, though, with cosmetics when you're older and that's the difficulty in getting eyeliner, lipstick and whatnot to remain in place, enhancing and defining your features instead of smudging and melting into an approximation of a Francis Bacon oil by the time you glance in a mirror a couple of hours later. Getting it to look right in the first place, on the days I do decide to wear it, is also getting a bit harder with the passage of time – age accelerates all manner of things. Eyelashes can all but disappear after menopause, ditto eyebrows; lip lines will crease (especially if, like me, you've been a dedicated smoker) and the lips themselves grow thinner; eyelids droop; noses get longer and so do ear lobes; our skin often improves but is much thinner and finer and more prone to damage; I refuse to call my freckles 'age spots'. Why should it matter? If you want flawless skin, you can buy it in a bottle. If you want long lashes you can buy those in a bottle too, or have extensions applied to your own. You can buy primers, CC cream, BB cream. You can, in short, re-plaster your skin and paint on whatever face you wish you had but where do you stop? If your face is now as flawless as a Spode china cup, then what about your neck? Do you make that flawless too, do you carry on down into your cleavage? And what about all the maintenance? Do you have your eyebrows waxed? Or threaded? Do you shave/epilate/depilate your face as well as your pits, legs, toes and bikini line? And what about those weird wiry badger bristles that you never notice until they're a couple of inches long? Do you have facials, pedicures and manicures? A spray tan? The look *de nos jours* for women in 2015 is 'porcelain doll' – how does *that* fit with a middle-aged face?

Over the years I've tried no end of things, new and old, and some were more successful than others. Once, at the Edinburgh Festival, I had fabulous 2in-long eyelash extensions just at the outer corners and they looked wonderful, but they were also a right faff. They got tangled in my fringe; they made applying my customary eyeliner a nightmare; they stuck to my sunglasses. I picked them off on the train journey back to London. I've had my eyebrows waxed (mildly painful), I've also had them threaded (agony) and I've had them tinted – especially now they're mouse grey – none of it is what could be described as essential but visible eyebrows are the one thing that make a huge difference to my face, providing a sort of punctuation to middle-aged soft focus. I have, on occasion, applied a little foundation to my chest area when I've been wearing a low-cut dress and it does make everything look a little smoother – not different, just better. I occasionally have a manicure and/or a pedicure but this is by way of a pampering treat, as is an occasional facial or massage.

Otherwise, what do I do to maintain myself? Very little, actually – I do not make my face smooth and eggshell-like because life is too short and I have less of it left than I used to. I do use a primer (which sounds as though I'm painting the kitchen door but stops an epic flush wrecking all my hard work) and I top it with a tinted moisturiser, a dab of blusher, some mascara and lipstick but not every day. My normal every day look since I stopped going out to work is *sans maquillage*. There are selfies out there in Internet land to prove that on many days I actually can't be arsed. There are also pictures of me with my normal made-up face – slightly rough around the edges, occasionally looking a bit of a spanner, but recognisably me and the me that I like and I'm comfortable with. Consequently I no longer mind seeing my photograph here and there and any selfies I post are not to brag about my wonderful opulent lifestyle – if you think I have one of those you've not been reading this book properly – but simply to put an older face up there with all the other much younger faces, to try and redress the balance a bit. I think we *should* redress the selfie balance. I think we should all be putting our pictures out there and reminding people we're here.

Maintaining my façade is one thing but the structure underneath is beginning to show signs of subsidence. Some days I feel a bit like St Paul's Cathedral – watched anxiously for bits dropping off. The most recent of these was my right retina.

I laughed out loud when the consultant says this can 'happen spontaneously as a result of wear and tear', which is doctor-speak for *you're getting on a bit and should expect these things*. I woke up one morning with something like a squashed beetle in the middle of my bedroom ceiling, realised it was in my eye and thought, 'Ah, there's a splodge of mascara in there' and ferreted about a bit with the corner of a tissue, but it wouldn't budge. It didn't budge with eye drops either, so three frustrating days later I went to my GP who winced when I told her about the poking about part and packed me off to the local hospital where the doctor explained that the retina on the back of the eye is rather like sticky tape and as you get older the sticky bit can wear off and then the retina starts to peel away. No, it wasn't painful, just annoying because I couldn't see properly. I had it zapped with a laser and it's all right now, apart from the 'debris'. Sometimes I'm looking at the sky as though through a tea strainer and sometimes a floater will drift across and make me think I'm being attacked by a wasp. I can't always quite see properly to put on my make-up and I worry that I might go out with clown spots of blusher, or a foundation tidemark, but I don't suppose it really matters all that much. And I've got a fantastic magnifying mirror. I bought a hefty magnifying glass too last year, when the small print on pill packets and hair dye got too small for me to read. My daughters think it's hilarious. Little griefs indeed.

Do you remember when you could breeze through life without knowing your doctor's first name because you hardly ever graced the surgery? When the only pill you took was the contraceptive one, or an occasional paracetamol? This is something about getting older I don't like at all, this feeling of being constantly under surveillance and fiddled with. High blood pressure runs in my family and I've got it too – I've had it for years and ticked along quite nicely with it until all that bother started a couple of years ago. Once I'd dug myself out of London my blood pressure shot up and stayed up (a physical manifestation of the toll a prolonged bout of catastrophe can take on an older body) and my new doctor noticed. So now I take *pills* for it – along with the HRT I've been prescribed since the hysterectomy (and have no intention of stopping because if I run out I feel like death and have to lie down for three days until everything returns to normal) and the anti-depressants that kept me on a reasonably even keel through more incidents and drama than your average Shakespearean tragedy. And there's the leg that drags slightly – courtesy of that ovarian tumour – the wayward cholesterol, a family history of heart disease and cancer, a recently perforated eardrum and a not-so-recently dislocated jaw together with all the usual twinges in back, hips, neck, shoulders, wrists and fingers that we all accumulate. It's just the effect of life on this 59-year-old body, a sign that I've lived a bit, and surprisingly I find I don't really mind it all that much. After all, I'm still here. And at least my brain's good – in fact, touch wood, my brain is better than it's ever been – it's just that when I sit down a bit heavily I swear I rattle.

What else can I do but try to love my ageing self a little and take care of me as well as I possibly can: eat properly, exercise often, lower my stress levels, rest when I'm tired and do my best to be happy. Although to be properly happy each human person needs certain things. Chief among those are a home, safety and finances together with a sense of purpose and self-worth (not so much Maslow's

Hierarchy of Needs, more an Invisible Woman's). In 2014 I was still struggling to secure at least three of those things.

By the middle of 2014 I'd come around to the idea of leaving London. I couldn't quite see how I would scrape together the funds I would need to move, but that didn't stop me browsing property websites for something, anything, that might work and it had to be a place I could afford on what I was earning now. I didn't want to go through this nightmare again and if I wasn't commuting and I was living on my own then I didn't need much. And I wanted to be back in the countryside ... I *longed* to be back in the countryside.

Then one day I found it – the one. As soon as I saw it I knew it was right: a tiny stone cottage in a Rutland village I knew well, on the opposite side of a valley to the house where I'd brought up my girls and where we'd been ridiculously happy. I might be able to afford it – I *would* be able to afford it, if I could somehow spread costs out a bit, only I couldn't get up to Rutland to see it. So I asked an old school friend who lived nearby if she would go and look at it for me and report back. When I opened the file with the photographs she'd sent and saw the one taken standing just inside the back door I burst into tears. There, dreamy through early evening sunshine, was a view I'd thought about pretty much every week since I'd left. I could smell the Rutland air. It's hard to describe what seeing that cottage did to me but it gave me hope and I knew it was for me so I said I'd take it. I had not the faintest idea how I was going to pack up and move north in four weeks' time, never mind the fact that I was moving from furnished to unfurnished, or that I didn't have a car when the nearest shop was miles away. Or that I still had a column to write and research to do. I was going home!

It's a funny thing but once I'd made that decision and set my course, the planets at last began to align in my favour and things began to go right, although they weren't finished with me quite yet. For now I just had to build up enough impetus to launch myself towards this new life.

8

The end of the beginning

*'You don't appreciate a lot of stuff in school
until you get older. Little things like being
spanked every day by a middle-aged woman:
stuff you pay good money for in later life.'*
—EMO PHILIPS

At some point, a very long time ago, our culture shifted from admiring and respecting older women for their wisdom, courage and resilience to vilifying, mistrusting and hating them. Worse is a culture that allows ageist misogyny to flourish and where women fail to support each other.

Walking through bustling Greenwich one sunny weekday morning I was followed by two men intent on upsetting me. Loud comments were made about my clothes, my hair and my appearance but mainly they seemed annoyed that I was, how should I put this ... not young. It was unpleasant but not worth making a fuss about; I'd heard worse. On the way down to the river we passed a party of uniformed schoolgirls on a study trip to the Maritime Museum and as we walked by them the comments behind me switched their emphasis from cutting me down to size to an animated discussion about which fourteen-year-old girl they would like to fuck and why. This made me angry in a way their baiting of me hadn't but I kept a lid on it until we reached the crowds by the *Cutty Sark*, where I stepped aside and suggested they go past me. I also suggested, politely, that they please keep their sexist remarks to themselves. For some reason that seemed to touch a nerve and I got the full hairdryer treatment with an off-the-scale outburst of sexist and age-ist insults beginning with:

'Shut your fucking mouth, you dried up old *cunt*.' (Lots of emphasis on the c-bomb.)

'Gosh!' I said, slightly startled, 'I bet your mum's proud of you.'

More followed, all along the same lines, all yelled at me (maybe they kept going because I stood my ground and didn't immediately burst into tears). Anyone standing nearby couldn't help but hear, several people even turned around, open-mouthed, for a bit of a gawp but no one – *no one* – came to help me or intervene. I'm only five feet two inches, these lads towered over me, but the general public carried on doing what they were doing and ignored the unpleasantness. Eventually they got bored and went away and I carried on with my walk. I was upset. It *was* upsetting. But what can you do?

That wasn't the first time something like this had happened. I'd been given a proper sweary mouthful by a couple of Army cadets for asking them nicely if they wouldn't mind putting their rubbish in the bin rather than chucking it all over Blackheath. They were sitting, in uniform, on a bench beside an almost empty litter bin, it wasn't a big ask.

Now contrast this with an incident one night in the early '90s at my local pub when a well-known twenty-something trouser-snake got ridiculously trollied and spent the night with the fifty-something barmaid. Everyone knew what had happened but nobody was rude to her and nobody laughed until she announced, quite magnificently, 'Well, at my age, if a bus is passing you hop on.'

What intrigues me most about the first and last of these stories is the changing attitude to the sexuality of an older woman. Can it really be that because I'm now judged sexually worthless (by whom?) I have no right to a voice or to express my own opinions? Could *that* be why middle-aged women find themselves pushed aside in the 21st century? Is the only valid currency the sexual kind? Surely that can't be right. That isn't what we worked for.

But what of the older women who have managed to escape the social cull and *have* fought their way to the top, the women who represent us in academia, in politics and in business? It seems they too get a raw deal. Pulled apart and held up for ridicule about their hair, make-up, clothes, weight, shoes or private life; for being 'shrill' (and told to 'calm down, dear'); for being too feminine or too masculine. It goes on to such an extent that we're more likely to see a headline about 50-year-old so-and-so's visible inch of outrageously exposed cleavage than why they disagree with a particular political theory or how they've turned a failing business around.

Certain sections of the media go on a gleeful hunt for decades-old pictures of a newly appointed Cabinet minister wearing not very much so they can push her back into a non-threatening role. As a woman, I never much minded Margaret Thatcher's 'Attila the Hen' moniker or her lampooning on *Spitting Image* – the satire was funny and clever and razor-sharp. I do very much mind seeing our female politicians reduced to crude misogynistic sexual stereotypes by cartoonists who almost never mete out the same treatment to male MPs. A parliamentary sketch writer in 2015 is more likely to froth over our female Home Secretary accidentally showing her knees on the front bench than her policies on immigration. But then I can't recall a female cartoonist or sketch writer in a daily newspaper, so I suppose that explains it.

We don't stick up for each other, we don't stick together, we've lost our sense of humour, we've stopped standing up for ourselves and we don't push back. Let's have no more of it.

At 50 we could, if we're blessed, have another 20, 30, 40, even 50 years of life. Are we only going to half live it? Perish the thought! My age now, for all its ups and downs, struggles and disappointments, feels very much like my prime to me – but then I thought I was in my prime at 30, then again at 40, and 50 was pretty damn good too. Perhaps we have different sorts of prime, at our different ages? Certainly I'm sure there'll be more of my prime to come at 60, 70, 80 … I hope I'll never think *that's it, I've done what I can, it's all downhill from here*. However hard it gets. After all, in the last two years I've reminded myself of something I'd forgotten: that down is not necessarily out and that down is usually followed by up.

Shortly before I moved out of London I heard that the book I'd been working on (*this* book) would be published. Once I had that news, the rest of the life pieces I'd been accumulating slotted into place. When my next-door neighbour told me he'd sold half his garden to developers and that work would shortly be starting on a three-storey house, moving out seemed even more urgent. Writing a book and living next to a building site are not compatible.

I still had the practical aspects of my move to organise but I'd said I'd do it and do it I would. No backing down. I booked two men and a van to move me, my books, a couple of pieces of furniture and Mr Pushkin Cat up to Rutland, to the cottage I'd never set foot in but had fallen in love with by email. I began packing.

The week before I moved, my stepmother died. Chemotherapy proved too much for her and she went downhill really quickly. I'd known her as my stepmother for longer than I'd known my own mother. In the middle of the moving upheaval it was hard to sort out exactly what I felt, and I parked it under 'to be dealt with at a future date'. It was another blow. I felt so very tired. I longed for some peace, for it all to be over.

Moving out of London felt like an escape and seemed an appropriate metaphor for this more recognisable shift into my middle age. On the threshold of 60 and a new career, poised to return to where I'd lived most of my pre-London life, it felt as though optimism was at last taking root. And thank heavens for friends. In all the time I'd been in London I'd been pretty self-contained but now when I needed it most, friends rallied round. Best of all was that the cat and I wouldn't have to travel to Rutland in the furniture van – a friend would drive us up. On a day that was sure to be an emotional one I would be able to let go of the stiff upper lip for once. I was relieved already.

The night before the move I suddenly started worrying that the van I booked wouldn't be big enough. Once I started pulling everything out of cupboards and from under the bed and behind chairs there seemed to be an awful lot of it. It was staggering what I'd accumulated over fifteen years in a flat the size of a large cupboard. As the boxes piled up the feeling got worse. At least 30 of the multiplying boxes contained my beloved books. I cannot be without books. I sold some once, when I thought I might be moving to Italy, and I mourn every single one of them.

When the removal men arrived the next morning they took one look and carefully explained that it wouldn't all fit. They could take the washing machine or the books, not both. It wasn't the volume, they said, it was the weight. Deciding to leave my books in London for a couple of days longer was agony. The cat attempted to remedy his own inner turmoil by making a dash for freedom but I rugby tackled him, boxed him up in his travel basket and left him in a quiet corner where he swore at anyone passing for the next two hours. My lovely friend came over with coffee, hugs, food and a willingness to muck in and help me clear up so that I wouldn't have to come back again.

Usually I feel sad to leave a place that has been home but not this time. The only things twanging at my heartstrings were the boxes of books I was temporarily abandoning in the hallway. When I walked out of that door the relief was indescribable and it felt as though a cloud was lifting.

In the real world the cloud was lifting too – the sun was shining. But you know that saying, 'it's not over till the fat lady sings'? Well, the fat lady had one more trick up her sleeve, as we discovered when my friend's new car cut out in the fast lane of the A14 just outside Cambridge. There followed two hours of sitting behind a crash barrier by the hard shoulder (with the cat hyperventilating inside his basket), a brief ride with the AA man and then another two hours waiting for lifts at the service station. And while all this was going on, my removal men and the inventory clerk were waiting at my new home, on a meter. I'd agreed a blanket fee up to a certain time limit, with anything over that being charged at a half-hourly rate. Given the state of my (non-)finances this was extremely worrying.

But I got there in the end. My daughter drove out to collect me (and the cat), the AA came to collect my friend and her car and we set off again, but this time in different directions. I finally arrived at the cottage five hours late and full of apology to find happy removal men who had unloaded everything, put it all where it was supposed to be and, because they had nothing else to do, plumbed in the washing machine. Now they were enjoying a cup of tea and a slice of cake provided by my new neighbours. They wouldn't accept any money for the extra time because, as they explained in broken English, it wasn't my fault and it wouldn't be fair. And that piece of kindness meant that I could book them on the spot to collect my boxed-up library from the flat and reunite us in Rutland.

That first night in my new home I opened a bottle of whisky and bedded down on the sitting room floor, wrapped in a duvet. The cat, filthy and dry-nosed, pressed in as close to me as he possibly could and we both slept – after a fashion, because there's nothing like new night-time noises and a fear of spiders for preventing peaceful sleep, however much single malt you've drunk. Two days later my books arrived and we were in. Almost.

We were a bit short of things to sit on and sleep in, not to mention storage. The only furniture I had was six bookcases, one chest of drawers and a washing machine – no bed, no table, no chairs and no cupboards. Perhaps more importantly I had no car. The first time I walked to the nearest market town nearly killed me. I had my laptop to work on but nowhere to sit and write, although it *was* beautifully quiet and achingly familiar. Heal first, I thought, and catch up with the rest later. There's no rush.

It took me some time to succeed at the healing bit. The cat bounced back quite quickly. I couldn't make it to my stepmother's funeral soon after I moved. That saddened me but it was time to admit that I needed to stop for a bit, that I couldn't do everything.

It was funny to be back in Rutland again because I had never imagined myself coming back – I walked through ancient woodland I last walked through 20 years ago and retraced my steps to the fishponds, a favourite tree, the badger sett and the brook. I visited a young friend in a sunny corner of the village churchyard and remembered the November day we'd all stood on the path, shaking our heads, inconsolably sad, my elderly American friend in an old pinstriped suit sharing a pack of cheroots. Such a lot had happened since then, and being aware of that kind of put everything back in its place and in the right order.

I've thought about this age thing a lot over the last couple of years and even more in the six months since I left London and it seems to me that there is a rightness and purpose to this business of middle age. I'm now in my 60th year, two-thirds of the way through my revised definition of middle age, and I've settled into my skin and bones – almost *grown* into them. I am on my way to achieving something I always wanted to achieve but had always found an excuse not to attempt. I'd allowed fear to hold me back. Whether writing will keep me in my old age or not remains to be seen, but at least I'm doing it, or learning how to do it (it's much harder than I thought). I'm giving my ambition a fair crack. Would it have happened sooner if I'd held out for university 40 years ago? I don't know and I think it's best not to go there – it's this future that matters and not that alternative one. I can stop fighting with my past and I can promise myself a future because I sure as hell know that I can get through most things. This is what *my* middle age has taught me.

Every good story has a beginning, middle and end. The middle bit is the meaty, substantial part, the part where everything comes together. If you want your story to be a thriller, then write yourself a thriller. If you hanker for something more lyrical then write that. Personally, I'm glad I've had a rough couple of years – glad because throughout all the ups and downs I've carried on learning new things and reminded myself of quite a few things I knew already but had forgotten. I have followed Lester Burnham's advice and surprised myself. If it was the case that I was drifting through my middle age in a fog of complacency and missed opportunities then the last two years have knocked some sense into me.

I am determined that I will not waste any more time on *what if*s and *what now*s. I will concentrate instead on *how can I ...?*

I have remembered that youth is relatively short-lived and there's an awful lot of life to be got through after it, and actually, that's all right because there are many, *many* compensations.

And speaking of 'youth', I am really, truly, honestly not jealous of younger women *at all*, despite being told that I must be. Who wants to go through all that again?

I know that I do admire beauty when I see it, although sometimes it makes me feel a little bit sad and wistful because it isn't the be all and end all and we will all have to learn that beauty changes its face according to its years and cannot be defined as any one thing. (I thought we did know this, once.)

It feels a bit odd when your grown-up daughter sends you food parcels but it's only because she's worried that you're not eating/can't afford to eat properly and it means you should be proud because obviously and in spite of everything you did a good job raising her on your own.

On the other hand, the grown-up children will still come and tap you for a few quid if they need it. Above all, this arrangement should now be reciprocal.

Not all social media is an instrument of the devil. There are a great many wonderful, funny, supportive, brave, remarkable women *of my age* out there and via the medium of Twitter we can all sit down together of an evening and exchange thoughts about *Countryfile*, muse about inanity, be properly and correctly cross about sexism and bad behaviour, live tweet *The Archers*, post cat pictures ... occasionally we will even meet up and like each other a lot. So it can in fact widen your circle of friends and your support network a long way beyond your immediate geographical vicinity. That is a good thing.

Persistence pays off and it's worth pushing on with something if your gut tells you it's the right thing to do, even if everyone else thinks you're just a batty older woman. And that's another thing. We need to disrupt that way of thinking about us.

Whistler's mother was only 65 when she was painted as a stooped, grey old lady. I'm five years off that and nothing like it. We are not our mothers. I do not want to see any more insulting stereotypes of drab, slow-moving, slow-thinking older women (or men).

Acknowledging that you no longer have a bottomless reserve of energy to call on does not mean that life is over but it does mean that when you're tired you should stop and rest. This is not giving up – it is looking after yourself.

Sleeping on the floor for four months in an old Rutland cottage is no good at all for this middle-aged woman and a slightly extravagant bed purchase is a perfectly appropriate reward for having survived said four months. I no longer enjoy roughing it and it gives me backache.

We do not always know what we like …
But we do know what we need.
What we need is not what we're getting …
But we can change that, if we try.

ONWARD!

Further reading

'Rethink, Rework & Act', The Age of No Retirement, 2014

Middle Age: A Natural History, David Bainbridge, Portobello Books, 2012

The Vagenda: A Zero Tolerance Guide to the Media, Holly Baxter, Rhiannon Lucy Cosslett, Square Peg, 2014

The Female Brain, Louann Brizendine MD, Bantam Books, 2007

'The Intersection of Gender and Age: Becoming a Woman Olderpreneur?', F. Colgan, H. Farnworth, K. Kalsi, A. Reynard and F. Tomlinson, 2008

'The Gender Gap in Pensions in the EU', European Commission, 2013

The Change, Germaine Greer, Penguin, 1991

Beyond Mid-Life Crisis: A Psychodynamic Approach to Ageing, Peter Hildebrand, Sheldon Press, 1995

Bomb Girls – Britain's Secret Army: The Munitions Women of World War II, Jacky Hyams, John Blake, 2013

'The Sandwich Generation: Older Women Balancing Work and Care', Institute for Public Policy Research (IPPR), 2013

How to Age (The School of Life), Anne Karpf, Macmillan, 2014

Essays in Persuasion, John Maynard Keynes, W.W. Norton & Co., 1963

'The Commission on Older Women – Interim Report',
    commissioned by the Labour Party, 2013

'Women Deserve Better: A Better Deal for Women Aged
    50 and Over in Employment', a Labour Research
    Department report for UNISON, 2014

How to be Alone (The School of Life), Sara Maitland,
    Macmillan, 2014

The Emperor of All Maladies: A Biography of Cancer, Siddhartha
    Mukherjee, HarperCollins, 2011

Ageism: Stereotyping and Prejudice Against Older Persons, edited
    by Todd D. Nelson, MIT (Massachusetts Institute of
    Technology) Press, 2004

Facing the Fifties: From Denial to Reflection, Dr Peter A.
    O'Connor, Allen & Unwin, 2000

'The Missing Million: Illuminating the Employment
    Challenges of the Over 50s', The Prince's Initiative
    for Mature Enterprise (PRIME) in partnership with
    International Longevity Centre (ILC), 2014

'The Missing Million: Pathways Back Into Employment',
    The Prince's Initiative for Mature Enterprise (PRIME) in
    partnership with International Longevity Centre (ILC),
    2015

'Maximising Women's Contribution to Future Economic
    Growth', Women's Business Council/Government
    Equalities Office, 2013

Acknowledgements

If you've read this far then it looks as though my personal reinvention and retirement plan has at least half worked. Thank you.

After working up to it for a good 50 years I have *finally* written a book, but I would never have managed it without:

The Tattooed Daughters – Fay, Holly and Josie. That they have grown into strong, funny, brave young women, wives and mothers has, I think, very little to do with me. They are wonderful and I love them.

I thank my lucky stars for leading me to Juliet Pickering, who has agented for me with patience, wisdom and cake. And for Kate Hewson who took a chance on publishing an Invisible Woman. At Icon I have to thank Duncan Heath and Robert Sharman, as well as Leena Normington and Andrew Furlow, for their hard work, meticulous editing and encouragement.

Without my friends and colleagues at the *Guardian* it's entirely possible that I would never have found my courage at all, so in no particular order (except for the boss, obviously): Alan Rusbridger, Georgina Henry ('FFS get it down'), Rosie Swash, Keren Levy, Katharine Viner, Janine Gibson, Helen Dagley, Giles Fraser, Sheila Fitzsimons, Jan Thompson, Aditya Chakrabortty,

Tom Clark, Madeleine Bunting, Michael Tait, Maggie O'Kane, Adam Freeman, Jane Martinson, Chris Elliott, Sarah Freeman – ta ever so for the experience, the opportunities, the education, the support and the lolz (of which there were many).

Thanks are also due to Mary Beard and Alison Moyet, and to Cari and Gigi at Gransnet, who have all provided inspiration, often without knowing it.

For helping to get me back to where I am now (content and in Rutland): Emily Blunden, Emma Mitchell, Lucy Parham, Harry and Suzanne Baines, Janey (Miss Pedigree) Manns, Liisa Hilden-Parsons (who photographed Younger Me) and Georgina Lee, who came through with a recommendation for a 'man and van' that surpassed all expectations. I offer my family – actual and step-, at home and abroad – a wry smile and heartfelt thanks for putting up with me, and any number of mad schemes.

There are extra squeezes for Mr Pushkin Cat who has endured a great deal but we kept each other sane with the assistance of catnip, salted caramel ice cream and single malt. He now has the 'grass under your paws' I always promised him.

My Invisible army of Twitter friends, cajolers, mopperuppers and supporters – you know who you are and you have my undying gratitude.

And finally, to The Aged Parent who never entirely lost faith but didn't quite make it to the end, I can say this: *I've done it, Pa.*